"...officer down, code three."

"...officer down, code three."

Pierce R. Brooks

Director of Public Safety, Lakewood, Colorado

Edited by
Paul D. Shaw
Editor and Publisher, Assets Protection Journal

MTI Teleprograms, Inc.
3710 Commercial Avenue
Northbrook, Ill. 60062

". . . officer down, code three."

First printing September 1975
Second printing January 1976
Third printing March 1976
Fourth printing November 1976
Fifth printing June 1977
Sixth printing February 1978
Seventh printing August 1978
Eighth printing April 1979
Ninth printing February 1981
Tenth printing December 1982

Library of Congress Number: 75-23841

ISBN 0-916070-01-8

Manufactured in the United States of America

Designed by Phil Hamilton

contents

1 the deadly errors — 1

2 missing the danger signs — 11

3 a silent alarm at the bank, code three — 43

4 sleepy sam — 63

5 dark nights, dark deeds — 75

6 the gun that wouldn't shoot — 99

7 to search or not to search—there should be no question — 117

8 the deadly combination: no search, no handcuffs — 147

9 taking a bad position — 157

10 tombstone courage — 171

11 a premonition — 187

12 beware of the "typical . . . average . . ." — 241

13 post-mortem — 251

14 glossary of terms — 265

the deadly errors 1

the deadly errors   1

It is not an easy thing to do, to go to a police officer's funeral. Such a day is never "nice"—it is usually cloudy, or a chill wind is blowing, or a drizzling rain is falling. Even if the sun is shining, it is still a gloomy day.

While riding in the funeral procession of an officer I had known, I wondered—why? Why did this happen? I had known this man. We would say publicly, "He was a fine officer." To ourselves we would say, "He was a damn good cop." And he had a fine family (it seems they always do). But now that fine young officer was inside a flower covered box in the back end of a big shiny black limousine. And his family was huddled together and sobbing in the rear seat of another big shiny black limousine. Although I had read the detective division follow-up reports of the incident, there still seemed to be something missing.

Now we were walking across the lawn of the cemetery. My mind wandered once more. Why? Then I reminded myself of an old rule of thumb, long used by the police, that should provide an answer. For years we have subscribed to a six word checklist to insure proper preliminary and follow-up investigation reporting. While standing at the gravesite, I silently went through the checklist.

Who? What? When? Where? How? Why?

Perhaps a mental review of the facts as I knew them would provide the answer I sought. I thought to myself:

Who?   Patrol Officer Peter F. Scott

What?   Murder, first degree.

When?   2115 hours, four nights and three days ago.

Where?   Main Street, one hundred twenty three feet west of 3rd Ave.

How?   How the incident occurred had been reported by all the local news media, and in official department documents. Later, an official publication would publish a one paragraph summary of the event:

"The Metro City Police Department reported that a patrolman, white male, 27 years of age, was shot and killed after he had stopped a motorist for a traffic violation. The subject, a wanted parole violator, was later apprehended and charged with this killing."

Why?   That was missing. The *why* had not been revealed.

A few days after the funeral I located the detective who had investigated the Scott shooting. Only because I had known him for several years did I finally persuade him to reveal "why." There was no question that officer Scott had been careless in his contact with the subject. After the stop he had not, as was required, advised the dispatcher of his location and license number of the vehicle. Officer Scott had been warned repeatedly of his failure to follow this and other similar required procedures. Scott failed to see the colored plastic tape on the stolen vehicle license plate that had converted a seven to a one and an eight to a three. He was shot in the back while writing the citation on the hood of his police vehicle.

"None of this information is in your reports," I said.

"Hell no," the investigator responded. "Somebody might read it."

Published statistics and summaries of these tragedies are easy to find. They are usually brief and to the point. The "who, what, when, where, and how" have been documented and are readily available for review. But seldom, if ever, is the "why" made known.

I believe there is a reason, even though it is a sentimental reason, and one that I can easily understand. I have been to many police officer funerals—too many. The first one was too many. I know the feelings of the other officers as we sit in church and later stand at graveside. I know how the ex-partner feels, the close friend, the classmate. We all feel the same—even those who barely knew the fallen officer. We are a fraternity. A fraternity without the ancient Hellenic symbols. We are a fraternity of brothers; brothers not by blood, but by choice. We are a very close fraternity. This in itself is the primary reason the "why" is not revealed in most police officer murders.

Traditionally, in such cases, we, the police, have reported only those facts acceptable to us. Under the circumstances, it is much easier to say, "Our officer was shot down in an heroic attempt to . . .", or, "Our officer died without a chance . . .", or, "As the officer attempted to arrest (or question) the subject he was suddenly shot and killed without warning."

It is easier to avoid dwelling upon the "why." It is easier on the families, it is easier on the department and, most of all, it is easier on ourselves. In almost every instance of a police officer murder we have subconsciously (or consciously?) blocked out any thought that the officer might have erred. That the officer committed an error is really "why" he died.

We cannot continue to disregard unpleasant facts when police officers are murdered. Difficult though it might be, we must admit that many police officers who die in the field have made mistakes. Perhaps not intentionally, but an error nevertheless. An awareness of the most commonly made errors and constant alertness will, undoubtedly, greatly increase the officer's chance of survival in the street.

The following chapters relate those instances of which I have become aware during many years as a police investigator and administrator. Most of the police reports I have read of officers killed in the line of duty were merely a summary of "how" the officer was killed. "How" is always easy to determine. A good investigative reconstruction of the incident will almost always reveal the "how," and will usually reveal the "why." But it has been my experience that most often the "why" has been deliberately avoided and left out of the official report. "Why" the officer died is more important than "how." The "why" should be

4

discussed openly in a roll call and in an in-service training atmosphere to help prevent other police officers from committing the same fatal errors.

The purpose of this book, then, is to identify the "why" for the police officer, so he or she will stay alive by surviving on the street.

This book describes a series of incidents, each a "classic," a "classic tragedy." Each incident is somewhat different, since the dead officers had committed one or more of the several deadly errors known and recognized by experienced police homicide investigators throughout the world. To avoid embarrassment and for the reasons stated, the incidents related are disguised only as to location and names of persons involved. But the "why" is evident in each case.

Obviously, many good officers are killed each year, and sometimes there is no way the tragedy could have been avoided. The ambush slaying by the sniper is the best example. The cases cited in this book, however, fall into another category: the avoidable tragedies. Initially, years ago, a few investigators began to discuss and document the pattern of deadly errors (or deadly sins as they were called then) that led to avoidable police officer murders. A lecture series soon developed entitled "Police Officer Field Survival." A recording of one of the lectures has been transcribed and appears in the next chapter, "Missing the Danger Signs." It was natural that, over the years, the topic was discussed by investigators of other cities and counties, then among investigators from other states and foreign countries. A remarkable coincidence was noted. In discussions with officers at seminars, schools, conferences, in court rooms and on extraditions, the problems, the deadly errors, were the same everywhere. Police officers were being killed unnecessarily and for almost identical reasons in all the states, as well as in Canada, Australia, South America, Mexico, Europe, Taiwan, Malaysia, South Korea and other countries. The "why," once correctly identified, was the same for police officers' deaths in all nations.

The list of deadly errors has not changed. The reader will recognize one or more of these fatal errors occurring in each of the incidents described in this book:

1). *Failure to Maintain Proficiency and Care of Weapon, Vehicle and Equipment*
If you have learned to shoot, will your gun fire when you pull the trigger? Will your car respond when you need it?

2). *Improper Search and Use of Handcuffs*
Many police fatalities here.

3). *Sleepy or Asleep*
How well can you react when you are?

4). *Relaxing too Soon*
Usually at those "phony" silent alarm calls.

5). *Missing the Danger Signs*
Miss or don't recognize them; they can be fatal either way.

6). *Taking a Bad Position*
Write a citation or an FI card with your back turned to the subject. Or, while confronting the barricaded gunman, be casual or curious from your place of concealment rather than careful and cautious from a place of cover.

7). *Failure to Watch Their Hands*
Where else can the subject hold a gun, or a knife, or a club?

8). *Tombstone Courage*
Why wait for a backup?

9). *Preoccupation*
Worrying about personal problems while on duty may be the hard way to solve the problem.

10). *Apathy*
A deadly disease for the cynical veteran police officer.

How many of the deadly errors have you committed thus far in your career as a law enforcement officer? Be honest. I will confess to one of mine and discuss that unforgettable moment in this book. Both of us have really just been lucky so far. I agree a little luck is necessary for most police officers but it can be stretched pretty thin. Staying alert—always, and mixing good judgment and common sense with a little bit of good luck will go a long way toward insuring survival in the street.

missing the danger signs

2

missing the danger signs 2

The Setting

A large and comfortable 40 seat classroom at the State Law Enforcement Training Academy. There are 31 student officers in a class composed of suburban and rural police officers, deputy sheriffs and state policemen. Three are policewomen. All of the officers have at least two years of experience. The most experienced policeman in the group has worked six years in a large suburban department.

This in-service training course, 40 concentrated hours in one week, consists of:

Advanced crime scene investigation
Human relations
Constitutional law
State penal code review
Supervisory techniques
Social psychology
A four hour presentation on police officer survival in the street.

The following material was transcribed from a recording made during a part of the lecture presentation on police officer survival in the street.

Instructor:

I am going to take the better part of this morning to discuss an interesting case, and you are going to get involved. I am going to ask for your input at intervals so follow the action as I relate the story. From past experiences with similar classes, I know we will end up having a spirited and controversial session. I can tell you now that there will be strong disagreement among you before we break for lunch.

Before I relate what happened in this case I want to set up a hypothetical situation. This hypothetical case will be closely related to what actually happened.

Now, momentarily convert this classroom to the roll call room at your police station back home. All of you are on the day watch, all working patrol in one-man cars—except for you three young ladies, who would be working one-woman cars.

I'm your sergeant. I've read your beat assignments, a training lesson, and all of you have passed a uniform inspection. You all look pretty sharp. I'm just ready to break up roll call and send you out when the lieutenant walks in the room and says, "Better read this to them before they hit the street." He hands me a teletype, and says: "Couple of bad bastards. May be heading our way. After you read it, put it on the clipboard for the night watch."

"Okay," I tell the lieutenant. I take the teletype, glance at it and tell you to take some notes as I begin to read it aloud.

"This is teletype number 71-727 from the Springdale Police

Department (Springdale, you know, is a city about 250 miles south of our city).

WAREX two subjects, armed and dangerous. Wanted for assault to murder a police officer, attempted murder, robbery and escape.

Suspect number one. Herman George. Male, Caucasian, 55 years, six foot, 205 pounds, gray bushy hair, wears dark glasses constantly.

Suspect number two. Billy Ralph. Male, Caucasian, 51 years, five foot ten inches, 165 pounds, bald and shaved head.

Subjects serving time for murder and armed robbery escaped from State Prison at 0330 hours this date. At 0730 hours robbed small market in Springdale. Both subjects armed with shotguns and automatic pistols. Market owner pistol whipped, in serious condition. Springdale officer dispatched to unknown trouble call this location shot down by both subjects upon arrival. Officer's condition critical. Subjects last seen northbound, US 72, in a 1965 green over tan Mercury, Colorado plate Charley Boy Adam three two one. Vehicle believed stolen, unable to locate owner. Vehicle emits heavy exhaust smoke while accelerating.

Any information, for Lieutenant Hollingsworth, Springdale Homicide-Robbery team."

As I finish reading the teletype in our make believe problem the roll call room com line rings. I pick it up and listen, and then advise you that the lieutenant has just received a supplemental teletype from the Springdale Police Department. Their officer has just died as a result of the shooting.

Everyone is dismissed from roll call to go out in the field on patrol. All of you are in full uniform and each of you are in a marked patrol car, alone. You realize there is a good possibility the murderers are heading our way. I hope you've accepted the fact that they're to be considered armed and dangerous. Any questions at this point?

Student Officer:
What kind of weapons do we have in our cars for this problem? I know we all have sidearms but in my department we don't all get to carry shotguns. Do we have shotguns for this hypothetical case? I know we're going to meet those guys or you wouldn't be setting up this problem for us.

Instructor:
Right. You bet you'll meet them. For the problem, you all have shotguns available in your cars. You should have in the real situation too. Any more questions? Okay, if not I'll continue.

Now you're out on the street patrolling your city. You're driving east near the outskirts of town approaching a major intersection It's high noon, daylight, excellent visibility. Suddenly you hear a loud report, very loud and very close. You've been around long enough to know that's no cap gun and it's no backfire. That was a shotgun. You pick up speed and as you reach the intersection, this panorama spreads before you:

Diagonally across the street at a small neighborhood market on the southeast corner you see a frenzy of activity. There's a man down in front of the market. He's elderly, has on a short sleeved shirt, white apron, dark slacks. You're close enough to see a large bloody stain spreading below his belt. A woman, she's elderly too, is standing next to the man and screaming. Now she kneels down by him and holds his head in her lap. There are several pedestrians in the area, some are trans-fixed and motionless as statues, others are running in different directions, some into each other. Several notice you and begin to point frantically toward the car pulling out of the market parking lot at a high rate of speed. You look at the car, the two occupants, and note the license plate.

The car is a 1965 green over tan Mercury. It's throwing up clouds of black exhaust smoke. A real polluter. Both occupants are male, Caucasian, 50 years plus. You can easily see the shotgun in the hands of the baldheaded man in the front passenger seat. The driver looks back at you as he clears the market driveway and you note his bushy gray hair and dark glasses. It's easy to read the license plate on this bright and clear day. Colorado, Charley Boy Adam three two one.

Now, for the purpose of this hypothetical problem I want all of you to assume the following:

You've just come upon a robbery of a small neighborhood market. The owner has been shot down in front of his store and has suffered a grievous wound in the abdomen. The robbery was committed by the two men in the Mercury leaving the scene. The men in the Mercury are the two suspects referred to in the teletype I read at your fictitious roll call. Remember, they're wanted for escape, robbery, attempted murder, and murder of a police officer. My question to you, and this will start our rap session, is that you have only two ways to go: either to the fallen market owner, the victim of the robbery and shooting, or after the two wanted men in the car. Which way do you go?

At this point the tape is unintelligible and garbled. The class has become a beehive of verbal activity, and is totally involved in the problem. After about one minute the instructor inter-

15

rupts.

Okay, hold it, let's do this. There are thirty-one of you in this class. We'll be democratic and take a vote. Then we'll talk about it and I'll tell you what happened in the real case. But before you vote and we discuss this problem I want to let you know I will not take one side or the other. This is your problem to work out. From all the noise you made a few minutes ago, it's obvious you're split in your opinions. Remember, I told you that was going to happen. After your vote I'd like to hear from some of you. I want you to defend your position. I'll play the Devil's Advocate regardless of how each of you responds. Any questions?

Student Officer:
You mean you won't tell us the right answer?

Instructor:
I mean for now I won't tell how I would react. After I'm done with this lecture, if you remember, ask me again. For now I don't want to influence your decision.

Now the vote. Just hold up your hands. How many of you would go to the market owner shot down in front of his store?

Hands are raised.

I count thirteen hands. Thirteen of you would drive over to the man who was shot.

Student Officer:
I'd also be on the radio asking for help and an ambulance.

Instructor:
Good. But let's get a count of how many would pursue the

suspects.

Student Officer:
Should be eighteen if thirteen of us go to the man at the market.

Instructor:
It doesn't usually work out that way. I'll show you what I mean. Let's see the hands of those of you that would pursue the suspects.

Hands raised.

Okay, fourteen. Fourteen of you would go after the suspects and thirteen to the wounded man. That's twenty-seven in a class of thirty-one. That's what I meant. And that's why I count both sides. You've got four people in your class that are still parked at that intersection and won't go either way or just don't know what to do. You've got to do something besides sit on your fanny and watch all this happen.

Now, who wants to justify his or her decision . . .

Many hands are raised.

Yes, go ahead. What would you do?

Student Officer:
I'd go to the man who'd been shot.

Instructor:
Why?

Student Officer:
Well, in our first aid class much stress was placed on learning

17

how to respond to injury cases and help people who have been hurt.

Instructor:

Okay, but I've a question for you. You've now stopped your patrol car at the market and you get out. You go to the man lying down in front of the market. He's been shot in the gut with a shotgun. You can see his intestines hanging out a big hole where his belly button should be. What did your first aid instructor tell you to do for a wound like that?

No answer.

Somebody else. Justify your decision. Yes, go ahead.

Student Officer

It's our duty to protect lives, and to save lives.

Instructor:

Agreed, it's your duty as a police officer to protect lives.

Anybody else? How about the other side?

Student Officer:

I'd chase the suspects. I'd radio for an ambulance and keep after the guys in the car. It's also our duty to arrest criminals.

Instructor:

I agree it is your duty to arrest people like that. But are you going to let the man lay there and die?

No answer.

Anybody else? Go ahead—

18

Student Officer:

You agree with both sides. That we should go to the man who's shot and also to chase the suspects. How can you do that?

Instructor:

Listen closely. I said I agreed it's your duty to protect lives and also to arrest people like our two killers. I haven't said yet which way I'd go in this case. You can do both.

Student Officer:

But you would go one way or the other?

Instructor:

Yes, only one way. You can only go one way.

Student Officer:

Which way?

Instructor:

I'll let you know before I leave today. Anyone else with an opinion?

Student Officer:

I'd go to the injured man. I'd radio to the dispatcher and request a roadblock to capture the suspects.

Instructor:

Okay, but you're in a fairly large city. Just because the bandits leave going east doesn't mean they continue eastbound. Also, remember they're driving a stolen car. They can easily and quickly steal another. Then they're gone.

Student Officer:

Did something like this really happen?

Did some policeman have to make this decision?

Instructor:

Yes, it really happened and a policeman had to make that decision. There is a more disconcerting difference in the real story too, the victim was a police officer. Let's talk about it and see if the victim officer made any mistakes to set himself up. We can talk about it as I relate the incident.

First, I should describe the setting.

The police officer in this incident is experienced, about four to five years on the job. He's working patrol in a marked, fully equipped, police vehicle in a city of approximately 400,000 people. The officer normally works with a regular partner, but at the moment he's on patrol alone. His partner is testifying in early (7:30 AM) traffic court and a new policy has directed that in such a situation, the second officer, if not needed in court, continues on patrol as a report taking car.

At 0740 hours the officer responded to the waterfront area, Pier 13, and took a theft report. He cleared the call at 0815 hours and a few minutes later approached a major intersection in a northbound direction, eight blocks west of the city Receiving Hospital. The intersection was signal controlled and the policeman stopped for the red light. Traffic was medium, mostly eastbound towards the center of the city.

To repeat, the time is 0820 hours, 8:20 AM. It's a clear but cool summer day. On the northwest corner of the intersection there is a theater. It's closed and won't open until 6:00 PM. On the northeast corner there's a gas station under construction. Several men are installing the pumps. On the southeast corner a bank, its door closed. The bank opens for business at 10:00 AM. On the southwest corner there's a neighborhood supermarket. The market opened at 8:15 AM for customers. Employees have been inside since 7:30 AM getting set up for business and all the cash has been distributed to the various departments inside the market. Again, the time is 8:20 in the morning.

While waiting for the red light, the officer in the car glanced to his left and noted an old model car parked legally at the south curb next to the market and about two car lengths west of the crosswalk. The car, a 4-door, looked beat, it bore an out-of-state plate. Two men were in the car; both were middle aged and dressed in casual clothes. One was sitting behind the steering wheel, the other in the middle of the rear seat.

The officer wondered what they were doing. He guessed they were waiting, but for what?

The light turned green. The easy way to find out, he thought, was to ask them. He knew also he could get a couple of FI's to turn in since his sergeant wanted more anyway.

The policeman turned left and glanced at the tag as he went by. Colorado, Charley Boy Adam, 321, on a 1965 green over tan Mercury. He looked at the 6"x9" card on his dashboard. The plate was not listed on the hot sheet. As he passed the car he was momentarily puzzled as the seated driver stared at him, then took a long drink out of a pint bottle of whiskey. He noted that the man in the back seat remained motionless paying no attention to him, glancing neither right nor left as he drove by.

The policeman continued westbound, then turned left and entered the market's nearly empty parking lot. He circled the lot, drove back and stopped behind the parked car with the two men. The officer stepped out and approached on the driver's side of the car. Glancing at the man in the back seat who still ignored him, the officer leaned forward and said to the driver, "Let's see some ID."

"What kind?" said the driver.

"Driver's license, what else?"

"How about a social security card?"

Now, at this point, I would like some response from the class. What do you think the men are doing there? What are the obvious danger signs? What should the officer be particularly alert for? Has the officer made any errors up to this time? Go ahead.

Student Officer:
There's another guy somewhere. One in front and one in the back, that's not a normal way to sit in a car. There has to be someone else, probably robbing the market.

Instructor:
Okay, one in front, one in back. That certainly isn't normal. It should be considered a danger sign. But I'll tell you now, there was no third person. There was a reason for the strange seating arrangement, an insignificant one it turned out, but that doesn't matter. Their odd seating arrangement was different and should be considered a danger sign. One more thing, in a holdup, you'll find that in a three-man bandit team, two go in and one stays outside to drive, not one in a store and two outside in a car. Anything else?

Student Officer:
I think they're going to rob the market.

22

Instructor:
  Why?

Student Officer:
  It's the only place that's open. They're going to do something,
  that's for sure.

Instructor:
  Right. Remember again, you have an advantage, you know
  something is going to happen or I wouldn't be talking about it,
  but the policeman who was there that morning didn't know
  that. Question?

Student Officer:
  That guy that took the drink, the one sitting in front, that's a
  danger sign.

Instructor:
  Why?

Student Officer:
  It's just not normal, particularly in front of the policeman

Instructor:
  Absolutely right. That's another danger sign. Why do you
  think he did that? Why do you think he drank from the bottle?

Student Officer:
  He's trying to attract the policeman's attention, to get him to
  come over . . .

Student Officer:
  Or to set him up.

Student Officer:

Or he wants to warn him about something.

Instructor:

Good. All good observations and thoughts. How about the car, is it stolen or not?

Student Officer:

It wasn't on the hot sheet.

Instructor:

Right, but it was stolen. It was a cold plate on a hot car. That's an old trick. Pick a cold plate off a wreck in a junk yard. The pros try to find a wreck to fit the year and model of the car they have picked to steal.

What about the open conversation with the driver? Any comments?

Student Officer:

The guy wanted to show his social security card.

Instructor:

Right. Why? Think about it.

And how about the policeman? Did he forget to do anything at this point, as he's approaching the car?

Student Officer:

Yeah, he didn't call for a backup.

Instructor:

Okay, but you don't necessarily call for a backup every time you want to stop and talk to somebody. What else? He forgot something very, very important.

Student Officer:
He didn't call in the license number of the car.

Instructor:
Right. That should be a hard-nosed policy in every police department. One or two-man cars, excuse me ladies, one or two-person cars, should always call in license numbers and location. Don't forget location on every traffic stop. In my department, it must be done even for a motorist assist. If there's no plate or if you can't read the plate, our dispatcher sends the closest unit to back you up automatically. If the officer making the stop doesn't give a code for clear five minutes after the contact, a backup unit will be sent automatically to check and see if the unit is okay. I can think of a couple of cases where that information; license number, location and backup, if no response is received in five minutes, would have made a big difference. One case in particular. A friend of mine wrote a book about it. He called it, "The Onion Field."

Let's go on with our story. I'll review and remark about your comments and observations later. You've made some very good observations, not necessarily correct, but what is important is that they're good observations and because they're "out of normal" they become danger signs. I'll explain what I mean by that later.

The officer, still trying to get the driver to show some I.D., now became more interested in the man in the rear seat, whose only movement was an occasional blink of his watery blue eyes. The officer's attention was focused on the jacket spread over the man's lap and both his hands and forearms were under the jacket. "What do you have under the jacket?" he asked. There was no response. A bottle, thought the officer, but this guy isn't dumb enough to show it like the driver was.

"Let me see your hands." This time a more firm request from the policeman.

Still no response, not even a glance at the officer. A car drove by and parked at the curb ahead of the green and tan Mercury.

The policeman walked around the rear of the car to get out of the traffic. The front passenger door opened in the car that had just stopped ahead and a little girl, nine years old, stepped out. "Get a dozen," said the lady in the front seat as the girl ran into the side door of the market marked "Bakery."

The man behind the wheel of the Mercury watched the officer's every move as he walked up on the sidewalk, then forward. He leaned down and again said to the man in the back seat, "Let me see your hands—lift up the jacket or get out of the car." Still no response from the man sitting in the back seat. The officer then opened the rear door and said, "Okay, out of the car."
Finally the man moved. He slowly slid across the rear seat toward the open door, but the hands and jacket remained as they had been. He moved very slowly and deliberately.

As the man reached the edge of the seat and started to swing his legs out of the car, the officer stepped back. Now the warning bells started ringing louder. He might be holding a bottle or even some grass, thought the officer, or it could be . . . the officer reached for his gun, but too late. The sawed off shotgun came up from under the jacket as the man rose from his sitting position. He pushed the muzzle of the gun against the officer's stomach and pulled the trigger.

The muffled blast lifted the officer off the ground and slammed him against the north wall of the market. A moment of quiet,

26

then a pandemonium of sounds echoed the explosion of the big gun. Screams from nearby pedestrians and from the young mother sitting in the car just ahead of the fallen officer, the screech of locked wheels on passing cars as the drivers braked and stared, the squeal of tires on asphalt as the green and tan Mercury pulled away from the curb and started to turn south at the intersection and the sound of a motorcycle, louder as it approached from the north.

Now down and on the sidewalk the young policeman freed his gun from its holster. He was in a sitting position with his back to the wall. He was surprised as he felt no pain even though he could not move his legs. As his assailants turned the corner broadside to him, he raised his gun to fire. The he saw the little girl, unmoving and transfixed in a position on the sidewalk not ten feet in front of him but between him and the car.

"Get down, get down," he cried out, then thought to himself, she looks so much like my own little daughter whom I might never see again. "Get down," he shouted, but the car was almost around the corner and the girl was still in his line of fire.

The officer lowered his gun, tried to holster it, but could not. Then he looked down and was surprised to see his intestines on the top of his left pants leg. Carefully, he picked up the loose intestine and tried to place it inside the bloody hole under the remains of his Sam Brown belt. He heard a shot. Looking up he saw a policeman on a motorcycle fire a second shot in the direction of the fleeing car. The wounded policeman's eyes closed and he fell backwards on the sidewalk.

When the shotgun was fired at the patrolman, a police sergeant, a supervisor in the Traffic Enforcement Section, was proceeding south about fifty yards north of the intersection on a fully equipped two-wheel police motorcycle. He was in regulation uniform and armed with a six inch.38 caliber revolver.

Recognizing the blast as that of a shotgun the sergeant sped up and reached the intersection just as the suspects' car had cleared the curb and was beginning to turn on the southbound arterial.

The police sergeant knew immediately what had happened. The policeman, he could see him, had been shot down by the men in the green and tan car leaving the scene. It appeared to him that the wounded officer was going to shoot at the men in the car but could not or did not in fear of hitting one of many passersby, particularly a little girl who was standing motionless in front of him.

The sergeant stopped and without dismounting completely, drew his revolver and fired two shots at the vehicle as it turned the corner. He then accelerated, crossed the street and parked at the curb next to the unconscious policeman. Several persons knelt at the wounded man's side, one placing a blanket over him as the sergeant called on his radio for help, an ambulance, and transmitted the suspects' description and their direction of travel.

Now, any comments from the class, what do you think now?

Student Officer:
The sergeant was right. He had to go to the policeman to help him.

Student Officer:
Particuarly another policeman.

Instructor:
Should there really be a difference? If you're going to help, is

there a difference in helping a wounded civilian and a wounded policeman? Think about it.

Now, I just want to see if this story has made a difference. I want to take another vote. How many would do what the sergeant did, go to the aid of the wounded policeman?

A show of hands go up.

Well, quite a difference. Some of you have changed your mind. I count twenty-two hands.

Now, how many would pursue the suspects? How many say the sergeant was wrong?

Fewer hands are raised.

Okay. Nine of you. At least now I have all of you doing one or the other, no more lackadaisies in this class.

Let's take a fifteen minute coffee break; when we return we'll critique our case.

Fifteen minute coffee break.

Instructor:
What we're going to do now is a very important part of your training as a police officer. The case critique. There are two kinds, the pre-trial critique and the post-trial critique. Let me digress a minute to explain. You should get into a habit of playing the Devil's Advocate in almost every case you investigate, particularly the important ones. My partner and I used to do it and it helped considerably. First, the pre-trial critique. Let's say you are working a robbery-murder. You have arrested the suspect, cleared the case and are now standing by to

go to trial. Prior to the trial, sometime before the prosecutor is ready to put on his case, you should sit down, review the case and take the side of the defense. Ask yourself, "how can I beat the case? Where are the weak points? If I were the defendant, what would I do to get off, even to lie where the cops don't seem to have much proof. If I were counsel for the defense, what would I look for to introduce into evidence for my client? Do I have a surprise witness? Or, a legal loophole to use to get my client off?"

Write it all down. Beat your own case. After you've done that, and given it a real honest try, go back to being the investigator and go over your case and do what you can to strengthen your case. Patch up all those weak points. It may be that you have more evidence to obtain, witnesses to talk to, lots of things yet to do. No police investigation is completed when you're ready for trial. The investigation is complete when the case goes to the jury, or the court, for their adjudication.

Then, after the trial, the post-trial critique. A critique after the trial doesn't mean a victory celebration in the local detective bureau pub. It means truthful, constructive criticism of your investigation, regardless of the outcome of the case in court. It is a complete, I emphasize complete, review of the whole case. All the events that occurred, the investigation at the scene, the reports you made, the arrest, the statements you took, the trial. The whole thing. After it's all over ask yourself these three questions:

What did you do you should not have done?

What did you not do you should have done?

What would you do differently if you were to work this case over again?

30

Pre-trial and post-trial critique, done honestly, will make any good policeman a great investigator.

Let's start now by following that golden rule of investigation and critique the case we've been talking about. Some of you have already mentioned some possible errors made by the downed policeman. Let's review and critique them.

First, the officer might have been less alert in recognizing danger signs because of his preoccupation with just writing two F.I. cards for his sergeant. There's nothing wrong with writing F.I. cards. That's part of the job and good patrol officers do it all the time. But you must remain alert for other things, particularly the possible danger signs. Preoccupation, or getting tunnel vision while on patrol, can be fatal.

You mentioned he didn't call in with his location and report the subject's license number. Again, that is so important. All police officers, big cities, towns, suburbs, sheriff's deputies, state patrolmen, all of you should call in the location and license plate if there is one, on any stop you make for any reason. That's a healthy habit to get into.

How about the officer's position just before he was shot? The shooting indicates the officer was standing just outside and centered with the door the subject was going to exit. He didn't have much of a chance standing there. He should've been behind the subject, towards the rear of the car, but in a position to watch the hands. Then he has a chance. If he's alert, he can easily get the drop on the subject. If he's in a good position it's almost impossible for the suspect to exit the car without exposing himself or revealing that he's carrying a weapon.

Remember, get in a position to watch the hands. Failure to watch their hands is one of the deadly errors. *Watch their hands.* That message should be printed on the walls of every police station in the country. Better yet, of every police station in the world. Where are the guns when they are fired at policemen? Where are the knives held when police officers get stabbed? Whoever got shot with a gun that wasn't in the suspect's hands? It just makes good sense. Until you have everything under control, *Watch the hands.* That's where it's going to come from if you're going to get it.

Regarding danger signs: be alert for things that don't look right. Ask yourself what's out of place. Why is that something missing? Or, why is something new there? Look for the "out of normal" condition. Be particularly careful if there are lots of little things out of place. That could mean one big problem.

In our case we have many danger signs. One man in front and one sitting in the rear of the car. That's a danger sign. An out of state plate, no luggage seen in the car. That's another danger sign. The car parked next to a big market; not a sign by itself, perhaps, but with others it could be a danger sign. The stall by the driver at the request for an I.D. There's a reason he's stalling and that's a danger sign.

The suspect drinking in front of the officer. Why? You all missed the reason, and again that isn't important. What is important is that it was done—a very definite danger sign. The suspect drank in front of the officer because he was nervous. The whiskey bolstered his courage before the planned holdup and he unconsciously drank from the bottle when he saw the policeman.

The man sitting in the back seat. His actions are definitely unnatural. The driver was an extreme in over-reaction to the presence of the officer; the man in the rear was an extreme in under-reaction. Both are danger signs.

32

The rear seat suspect's refusal to move and to show his hands has to indicate a potential problem. He's holding something he doesn't want the officer to see—another danger sign. Be prepared for the worst.

All of the above are danger signs. All are things "out of normal." One by itself might not mean much, but all together, get ready—something's wrong.

Yes, question?

Student Officer:
Why was the guy sitting in the back?

Instructor:
I'm coming to that. It goes with why they were there. The real reason has little to do with the case. The right front door of the old car was sprung and jammed shut. There was a reason the suspect wanted to get out fast and on the right side, so he had to sit in the back.

I threw you a curve when I first explained the setting and the location. Remember the buildings on the corner? The movie was closed and therefore not a target; the gas station wasn't even built yet. The market was a possibility, but the best hit time was gone because the money has been scattered all over the market to the different vendors. What was on the other corner?

Student Officer:
The bank. But you said it wouldn't open until 10 o'clock, and all this happened before 8:30 in the morning.

Instructor:
Correct, though I said the bank opened for customers at 10

o'clock. The bank employees started arriving shortly after 8:00 in the morning, something all of you should remember. Remember, we have a couple of real pros; these two are experienced holdup men and have graduated to banks. Their M.O. is to watch the opening procedure and go in early with no customers to bother them. They were waiting for the last of the employees to arrive. Then they'd drive across the street and the robber in the back seat would get out quickly and show the shotgun to the employees at the door. He'd then go in and keep the others covered until his partner parked the car and walked back to the bank to be admitted. Then they'd take their sweet time looting the place. But the young officer interrupted their plans. They were a couple of losers, and real bad guys. To them it was the lesser of two evils; take a chance and shoot the cop and get out of town, or surrender and go back to a certain long, long jail term.

Now let's discuss our controversy. Which way do you go? To the injured citizen or policeman, or do you pursue the suspects? At last count, you were twenty-two to nine in favor of going to the wounded officer.

Before I tell you what happened, there is something else you should know. One of you mentioned that you would help the police officer and put out a description of the suspects and they would be trapped in a road block. That could be, but not always. In this actual case, the suspects escaped from the scene. The motorcycle sergeant did not choose to pursue. Hundreds of road blocks were thrown up. City police, other neighboring suburban police departments, sheriff's department and state police, all were involved. Several thousand police officers were looking for the cop shooters for days.

They were finally identified and apprehended more than four years after the incident occurred. Later they admitted the shooting. Think about that for a while: more than four years later.

Now, a subject of great controversy: to pursue the suspects or assist the injured policeman? The sergeant in this case was suspended for a period of several days. Not for shooting at the suspect's car, but for failure to properly use the police equipment at his disposal in order to prevent the escape of the dangerous suspects. Was it controversial? You bet it was. Even in that department. What do you think?

Student Officer:
You mean the sergeant should try to arrest two guys like that while he is on a motorcycle? What chance would he have?

Instructor:
No, he wasn't disciplined for not attempting the arrest. Any attempt by the sergeant to capture the two men by himself would have been another one of those classic and foolish acts I described to you yesterday as "tombstone courage." Since the sergeant had a motorcycle, the suspects couldn't have gone anywhere without being followed by the sergeant. He also had a radio; all he had to do was lay back and relay the direction of travel over his radio and the two men would have been, in a very short while, faced with odds of probably 50 to 100 to 1 against them. No, the sergeant wasn't disciplined for failure to attempt to apprehend the two men, he was disciplined for not assisting in setting up their apprehension. Nobody expected him to ride up along side of them on his motorcycle and wave them over to the side for shooting down a policeman.

I want to read from a training lesson printed many years ago by the Los Angeles Police Department. What I will read to you is but a part of a series of training lessons relating to police officer confrontation with armed subjects. This lesson is en-

35

titled: "Officer Shot—Suspects Pursued."

"Probably the most emotionally charged situation an officer can face is to see his partner or a brother officer shot down. This situation becomes more difficult as an instantaneous decision must be made: to pursue the assailants or aid the officer. Some prior thinking about this type of situation, before you are confronted with it, would aid you in making the right decision.

A decision must be made. The officer must either pursue the assailant or aid his brother officer. It is the position of this department that the officer has only one responsibility: to pursue and apprehend the assailant. At first this may seem a severe edict, but let us examine this type of situation:

"When you become a police officer, you assume the responsibility to pursue.

"If the suspects escape, they may never be apprehended or will assault others who resist them.

"No one is as qualified as a police officer to pursue and apprehend such vicious criminals.

"Other persons are as well or better qualified medically to aid the wounded officer.

"If other persons are present, they can request aid.

"If no one else is present, you can request aid on your radio while pursuing the suspects.

"Criminals must understand that they will be relentlessly pursued by Los Angeles police officers."

Instructor:

Earlier, you asked me what I'd do in a similar situation. I'm a product of the environment I became accustomed to as a police officer; the training I received, and peer group association. Instinctive reaction and personal beliefs are also factors in my behavior as a police officer, as they are and will be in your behavior as police officers. I concur with the policy as stated in the training lesson. I would pursue.

Let's think a minute about our case, the one we have discussed this morning. Many of you said you'd go to the person who'd been shot rather than pursue the suspects because you had a duty as a police officer to protect lives. I agreed. But I agreed that you have a duty to protect people generally. Now as you approach the scene we described you are suddenly aware that a citizen or a police officer has been shot down by armed subjects who are attempting to escape. At that instant, where is the greatest threat to society and human life? Where is the greatest danger? It seems to me that you might be thinking to protect or to save lives in the medical sense, not as a police officer. At that point in our story the greatest threat that you must deal with in order to protect lives is to insure the apprehension of the subjects who have already killed and injured several persons and who will surely do so again if allowed to escape.

In closing, I want to remind you of what I said when I began this talk. I'm just sort of a story teller; a true story teller of some things that have happened to other good policemen who might have gotten careless for just a moment or two. What happened to them I hope will never happen to you. That's why I told you the stories. This subject is not like others where you have rules and regulations you must follow. None of you work for me. I have no right to tell you to do things one way or another as they apply to the subjects we have just discussed.

You do your thing, whatever you think is right. Go to the injured citizen or officer, or pursue the suspects, but do one or the other. Do what you think is best, or what your Chief or Sheriff tells you to do. All I want you to do is remember some of what I told you. Stay alert and be careful.

I know some of the things I've said probably have upset a few of you, perhaps even angered some. It sometimes happens, particularly if you've known a policeman who was killed in the line of duty.

To answer a question one of you asked yesterday, yes I certainly do infer that most policemen killed by criminals died because they made a mistake. I make that inference for two good reasons. First, because in my experience I believe, regretfully, it's true. Second, I want to jolt you enough with it that, like it or not, you will remember what I've told you for a long, long time—as long as you are out in the street as a working police officer.

"...a silent alarm at the bank, code three"

3

"...a silent alarm at the bank, code three"

"All units in the vicinity and car seven seventy-six, a silent alarm at the Marine Bank, Main and Fifth Avenue . . . Car seven seventy-six, Code three."

The call came out over the police radio at exactly 0914 hours. The dispatcher, a woman with seven years experience, transmitted the information clearly and calmly as was her habit. Long standing department procedure required emergency response by at least one two-man unit. But times were changing. The necessity for emergency runs to silent alarm calls was argued at all levels in the Patrol Bureau. A month earlier, a two-man unit responding to a false robbery alarm at a savings and loan company had collided with a camper. Both officers and the four members of the vacationing family were seriously injured. Veteran police officers believed nearly all silent alarm calls were "phony."

An attitude, based on the fallacy that an unverified silent alarm was false, permeated the department. And behavior resulting from this attitude would have tragic consequences. This is the story of six men, of their attitudes and behavior and the tragedy that began with the radio call directing Car 776 to proceed to the bank at 9:14 on a hot Tuesday morning in August.

Sergeant Aloysius J. Adams was obviously uncomfortable as he drove his three wheeler south down the hill through the still heavy morning traffic on Third Avenue. He had his usual sweaty nervousness—he'd never really felt safe on one of those twenty-one horsepower tricycles. The already blazing sun promised the worst kind of physical misery for the remaining seven hours of his tour of duty. In fact, he thought, the day had started to go bad when he had walked into the station two hours earlier.

Just before roll call his wife had telephoned him at Traffic Control Division headquarters. She caustically reminded him of how many times he'd been warned to clean out the old water heater. Then she suddenly burst into tears and told him the bottom had rusted through, the basement was flooded with dirty reddish water and the two boxes of beautiful and expensive yard goods her mother had sent her were soaked and ruined.

Roll call brought up another on-going problem. It completely frustrated him to think that with all his seniority, almost 25 years on the job, the lieutenant still kept him outside in the field and had that new young sergeant sitting at the desk—by all rights his job. But Sergeant Adams knew the reason which only increased his sweaty aggravation. He was certain the captain and the lieutenant were conspiring to insure his retirement three months from now by making him work outside while knowing full well he wanted desk duty in the new air conditioned station. Well, the hell with them, he thought. Only 98 days and seven hours from now I'll be out because I want to be out. Besides the department had changed so much in the past few years he could hardly stand the place.

Seniority didn't mean a thing anymore and now there was all this talk about needing a college education to get ahead. What kind of a college could teach you to catch a burglar or spot a pickpocket in a crowd waiting for a bus? He had put plenty of them

44

in jail in the last two decades and the only time he had been on a college campus was to answer a call. And the so-called "new breed" galled him. Now that rookie with just a little over four years on the job was not only a sergeant but he was usurping Adams' rightful place on the desk. The lieutenant called it a part of "career development" whatever in the hell that was. But, come to think of it, thought Sergeant Adams, the lieutenant only had twelve years on the job. No wonder.

Glancing ahead at a row of parked cars he saw a curved violation flag suddenly fill the window of a parking meter. The sergeant noted the location and began to feel a bit better. Perhaps it wasn't going to be such a bad day after all. He slowed and as quietly as possible pulled into the open space between a compact and a new metallic blue Cadillac. The big Caddy was parked squarely in front of the meter flying the red flag.

Adams knew the car belonged to one of the many wealthy female customers that frequented Norman's *Coiffures de Normandy* beauty parlor. Maybe now he could get even with that miserable little fag. Norman had been the sole cause of his last three-day suspension and he remembered the incident clearly. Two months ago he had stormed into the *Coiffures de Normandy* to warn Norman about his loud stereo. Sergeant Adams did not like rock music and would not tolerate it on his beat even though no one had complained.

Tempers had flared and the sergeant called Norman "a dirty old queen" and his 17 year old clean-up boy "your fruity sweetheart." All this had occurred in front of a shop full of women customers. After the confrontation, Norman and several of the ladies present had complained—officially. Much to the sergeant's disgust the department didn't back him up. The three days suspension without pay really hurt and set him back a month on his boat payment.

Hell's fire, in the good old days he would have been the "complaining party" and a vice squad team would have tailed Norman and his young lover until they busted them for being sex perverts.

But now, retribution at last. He had to be careful though. The instructions he had received from his captain after returning to duty from suspension were very clear. The captain told him that, one, he was to stay out of Norman's place of business, and two, for the sake of good community relations he should always cancel a parking citation if the vehicle owner appeared before he had time to complete the citation or had cleared the area. He should also have a friendly "chat" with the citizen, the captain said, and advise them the citation would be cancelled. The thought of having a friendly chat with Norman or one of his customers was particularly revolting to Sergeant Adams.

The sergeant wrote quickly. He knew Norman absolutely guaranteed his customers freedom from parking fines by keeping his boy on the alert for red flags. When one appeared, a dime was instantly fed into the meter. But the flag next to the big Cadillac had not yet been noticed. Adams laughed to himself, "Mrs. Richbitch" would be plenty upset. And Norman would have to pay the ten dollar Central Parking District fine and maybe lose a customer.

He placed the hard copy of the citation under the windshield wiper and was getting back on the cycle when he heard the familiar shrill voice yell his name. Damn, too late, he muttered to himself, then thought: the hell with it. He looked around and saw Norman and the boy running towards him. Two women customers were watching from the doorway of the shop. With the throttle wide open he couldn't hear their voices but there was no doubting the words, ". . . tell your Captain," forming on Norman's lips as Sergeant Adams grimly steered the motorcycle out into heavy traffic.

46

There was only one chance to get out of this one, he thought, and he'd already made up his mind—lie. His only hope was to deny having seen or heard Norman and the boy. As he approached the bottom of the hill he braked hard and stopped just in time to avoid colliding with a car that had stopped for a red light at the intersection. Maybe, just maybe the captain might believe him if he'd strongly insist that he'd not seen or heard those people.

He knew the captain wouldn't suspend him if he had a reasonable doubt about the incident. What the hell, he mumbled to himself, that's what reasonable doubt is all about anyway. It happened in court every day. You gave a guy a ticket and if he was convincing in telling his lie to the judge, or the jury, he got off. A good lie was the foundation of establishing reasonable doubt—any traffic cop knew that. Trouble was, the captain wasn't as gullible as most traffic court judges. Problems, problems. He knew he was in for a good chewing out at least.

Sergeant Adams turned at the corner and drove west on Main Street. The plumbing shop was at 18th and Main and the owner, a retired officer and an old friend, would give him something off on the new water heater he was going to have to buy and install in his basement. He was at midblock when he heard the call on his radio at 0914 hours.

"Damn," he said aloud. He was talking to himself again. "More problems. That bank is just a couple of blocks down the street." He slowed down and pondered whether he'd be the first one there and have to wait in the heat for the radio crew car to show up. He decided he wouldn't go into the damn bank and listen to some teller put the blame on the alarm system rather than admit he'd been clumsy and had accidently tripped an alarm. Let the patrol car take the false alarm report. He'd just slow down for the next two blocks, time it to hit the red lights and everything would be O.K.

But it wasn't working out that way. As the light turned green at Fifth Avenue and Main, Adams realized he'd be the first at the bank.

"Where in hell is that radio car?" He grumbled and muttered to himself as he parked the motorcycle at the curb near the southeast corner of the bank. He thought how wonderful it was going to be someday when he could get up any time he wanted, take his boat and go fishing any damn time he pleased. No more riding in this damned heat, no more screwed up lieutenants, shitass captains, baby-faced sergeants, and best of all—no more Normans. At the moment Sergeant Aloysius J. Adams stepped slowly up on the sidewalk his cluttered brain had, for all practical purposes, completely blocked out the reason he was now standing outside the Marine Bank at Fifth Avenue and Main.

Traffic Enforcement Officer Bill Baker was enroute to the station when he heard the call at 9:14 AM. About twenty minutes before, at 0855 hours, he'd stopped a good DUI on his beat, the South Beltline Freeway. The district radio car had assisted him in impounding the drunk's car and was transporting his prisoner to the station. It was pretty early in the day for a DUI, he thought, but the guy had just drunk too much beer too early in this heat. The driver really had a snootful and would be an easy point two oh on the breathalyzer.

As the young motor officer listened to the call he decided the least he could do was swing by the bank and see what was happening. After all, the district car that would've responded, couldn't because of helping him with his prisoner. Baker turned north on Fifth Avenue. As he headed for Main he watched for pedestrian violators and vehicles late on the red light. He saw none. When he stopped for the red light at Fifth Avenue and Main Street he looked across the street and saw a sergeant stepping onto the sidewalk in front of the bank.

He recognized Sergeant Adams immediately. After working for him for over a year how could you forget that profile? Baker knew he was one of the very few young policemen that the cantankerous old Sergeant tolerated. He also knew it was because they were both avid fishermen and because he had more than once advised Adams of some good spots full of hungry bass. Baker wondered how Adams had made out with that last tip he'd given him. If Adams had had good luck there he'd give the lake a go himself tomorrow, his next day off and the first try at fishing for his five year old son. One way to find out, he thought: go ask him.

Sergeant Adams finally noticed Baker after he'd parked his motor behind the three wheeler.

"Hi kid. I see you still haven't cracked your skull riding that crazy machine."

"How's fishing?" grinned Baker. "How'd you make out at Lost Lake with those flies I tied for you?"

They discussed fishing as the wailing of the distant siren increased in volume.

Carl and David were good policemen. Their captain was pleased to have them, the lieutenant was glad to have them assigned to his watch, and the sergeant wanted them on his team.

Carl and David had asked to work together and were happy when their request was granted. Playing ball together for three years in high school, and the two more at the community college, had cemented their relationship about as well as might be expected for the all-conference shortstop and second baseman. Their families were also close. Each had married the girl next door, and all four were from the same neighborhood.

Joining the department had finally separated them, but now it had brought them together again. It had been a long wait, however. Within a half hour after their academy graduation, David had been told to report to Narcotics Division for an undercover assignment.

For the next two years he had lived in the rotten world of pills, grass, hash, coke and heroin. For two years he had bought junk from neighborhood pushers and, on four occasions, from mules who had carried large amounts of hard stuff across several international borders.

But enough was enough. It had been particularly rough on his young family. David's wife had presented him with two beautiful daughters. He was one up on Carl and he secretly hoped the next, due early the next year would be a boy, whom he would name Carl—as Carl had named his son, David, for him.

As Carl drove car 776 out of the station that Tuesday morning they discussed the surprise picnic they were planning on Friday for their families. The kids and the dogs would enjoy the outing. What a great way to celebrate the two of them finally getting together again. They'd be as good a team on patrol as they had been in the infield.

At 9:14 AM they received the call to respond to the silent alarm at Fifth Avenue and Main Street. The location was five blocks outside of their beat to the west. Carl remembered hearing a call that had been assigned the car in that district to assist a motor officer who'd stopped a drunk driver on the freeway. He turned on the red lights and siren as he turned west on Main Street

"No sweat," he told David, "this will be a slow code three. Probably a false alarm. The bank doesn't open for another 45 minutes anyway. Some teller has accidentally tripped a button again."

David nodded and relaxed. It was his first code three run and he watched as his partner carefully threaded his way through downtown traffic. As they approached Fifth Avenue, Carl cut the siren. David looked ahead and could see why. Two policemen had already arrived and were talking on the sidewalk in front of the bank. This was going to be easy, David thought, compared to some of the situations he had faced during his past two years as a narc. Both patrolmen stepped out of their cruiser and walked up to the sergeant and the motor officer.

Eddie and Frank had checked out of the old hotel on the southwest corner of Fifth Avenue and Main on Friday at noon. For five days they had cased the bank, carefully noting the opening and closing procedure. By Thursday, they knew enough to decide to make their hit the following Tuesday morning well before the doors opened for customers at 10:00.

The information on which they'd made their decision hadn't been solely the result of their patient fourth floor stakeout. Earlier in the month, while walking by a downtown shoeshine stand, Eddie and Frank had met an old ex-con they'd served time with in a Midwest state prison. Both of the younger men had been about to leave the old wino when he had mentioned an item of

51

great interest to them. Their attitudes changed immediately from bored indifference to fascinated attention. He had gotten a job, he told them, with a big janitorial company in the city. But his obsession for alcohol had eventually overcome his desire for steady work and he had been fired two weeks earlier. Fortified with this information, the rest was a natural for Eddie and Frank.

For several nights, the three went out to dinner. The old man was delighted and surprised that his two young friends were so attentive and generous. They hadn't been that friendly in prison. They ate well and drank good whiskey, particularly the old man. Eventually Eddie and Frank were told that the oldest and still biggest bank in the city had been visited many times by their old friend when he worked the night cleanup crew. Two dinners and many ounces of good bourbon later, Eddie and Frank had the floor plan of the bank and, most importantly, the location of two silent alarm buttons noted by the old con while he was cleaning up around the desks of the bank president and vice president.

During their five-day surveillance from the hotel the two robbers had watched a large armored car make a delivery late Monday afternoon. The number of employees had already been counted and the times of their arrivals and departures noted. The bank president had been easily identified: he was well dressed, owned a new Mark IV and was the last one to arrive at work. Eddie and Frank had watched as he parked his car in the lot next to their hotel, walked to the corner, bought a paper, walked across the street to the door of the bank, knocked and was admitted at exactly 9:08 every morning.

On Saturday night Eddie and Frank had completed another phase of their plan. They met their informant once more. Both knew he was still cunning enough to realize he was providing them with information on some sort of a job—most probably the bank they had asked him about. All three drove to the outskirts of the city for a big steak dinner. It was the last supper for the old ex-con. During dinner they talked of the good old days and jobs pulled in the past. Two stops and many drinks later, the last drink laced with two "reds," the old man fell into a drugged stupor while trying to finish the story of his biggest haul, a safe job in a St. Louis Post Office thirty years before.

One hour later, a little after 3:00 Sunday morning, the drunk old safe cracker was laid out on a switch engine spur in the city railroad yard. By 5:50 AM he had been decapitated and mutilated by three trains before his scattered remains were found by an early morning inspection crew.

On Monday evening Eddie had stolen a car for the robbery and parked it at their motel.

Tuesday morning they arose early and had a light breakfast. At 8:25 AM they both took long sniffs of white powder from an envelope that had been hidden under the front seat floor mat of their car. At 8:30 they parked the car a half block from the bank. Their only conversation all morning had been a mutual, drug-induced reaffirmation that in no way would they ever return to jail—any jail: city, county, state or federal.

At 9:06 AM they stood on the corner of Fifth Avenue and Main and watched the bank president park his car. He was right on time. They could feel the sawed off shotguns slung under their light weight jackets. The weapons were a bit uncomfortable, but reassuring.

They met the president at the door on schedule. Five seconds after the president knocked on the door to be let in Eddie stepped forward and pulled back his jacket. When the door opened, the three walked into the bank without notice.

The robbers went to work immediately and according to plan. Frank began filling two large bags in the vault while Eddie covered the nervous but very obedient employees, all of whom had been moved away from the two wired desks. After several minutes Eddie became impatient.

"Don't move," he said, then walked slowly by the small group passing the muzzle of his shotgun inches from the row of mute faces. He then turned and pulled open the first of a row of six teller drawers and began placing the money in a small bag. Even if he'd seen the trip wire it would've been too late, because he'd already removed the bait money from the drawer. It was a few seconds before 9:14 AM.

One and one-half minutes later Frank emerged from the vault pulling two large, full bags behind him. Eddie, shotgun always pointing toward the men and women standing motionless near the east wall, emptied the last drawer of cash. Both heard the siren at the same time. Faintly at first, and in the distance, but increasing in volume and coming closer.

"Check it."

Eddie nodded and walked to the front window and cracked the old venetian blinds. Almost without expression he looked back at Frank. "Two out front, two more coming up in a car."

Frank swore, grabbed two more bundles of bills and hurriedly stuffed them into a bag. Then he carried both bags to the front door. Eddie joined him. Without comment, but knowing what they must do, they opened the door, raised their shotguns, stepped out onto the sidewalk and began firing. They fired rapidly but deliberately at the four policemen while they stood talking, while they fell and after they were down. Guns emptied, the two men picked up the bags and walked quickly towards

54

their car.

On Friday, picnics had been planned for the two families. In stead there were funerals for the two families. The department chaplain, looking down at the two flag and flower draped caskets in front of him, eulogized, ". . . two of our very finest, they were students together, teammates together, police officers together and they have died together."

The funeral was magnificent. Almost two miles of slowly moving, red-light-flashing police cars and motorcycles from departments throughout the state led and trailed the procession to the cemetery. It included the Mayor, the Lieutenant Governor, a Congressman, and members of the bereaved families—all except David's mother, still in a hospital in deep shock and unable to comprehend the sudden tragic horror that had taken her only son. That evening, local TV newscasters again denounced the heinous crime.

Ten days later a small column on page 26 of the local newspaper mentioned that two suspects in custody in a large northern city had been eliminated as the murderers. Three weeks later a rookie policeman at the police academy, troubled by the stories of the shooting he had read and heard, stood in class and asked, "Sergeant, could you tell us how all of them were shot down like that, never able to draw their guns and get off at least one shot?"

The sergeant's reply was husky with emotion, "It was a set up. The killers came out of the bank and gunned them down as they arrived. They never had a chance. Now let's forget about it; I knew two of those men and it's not easy to talk about."

Four weeks later Officer Baker was allowed to leave the hospital and return home, though he would have to return once a week for therapy for many months. His left leg would be rigid for the rest of his life—almost a full charge of double-ought buck had removed his knee cap and had almost severed the leg. He would also have to learn to fish with the hook that was being ordered to replace his right hand, torn off when he had reached for his gun on that fateful Tuesday morning.

The story does have a happy ending—of sorts. Sergeant Aloysius J. Adams was happy. With the wounds in his hip well healed he had returned to duty inside, as Desk Sergeant in Parking Control Division. In fact, the sergeant was so pleased with his assignment he began to consider sticking around. Why retire when he had it so good? Besides, he thought, there's a lot I can teach these new young cops.

The training sergeant's response to the rookie's query is worth reviewing. The sergeant voiced the thoughts of law enforcement officers everywhere when he said, ". . . it's not easy to talk about." But as difficult as talking about it may be, we must discuss such incidents if we are to increase the chances for survival of our officers in the field.

It's obvious that the training sergeant was protecting his errant brother officers when he told the young officer, "It was a set up . . . they never had a chance." In a way he was correct. Analyze the case; all the facts, including the "why" are known. It was a set up. But who set up whom?

Certainly Sergeant Adams set up the other officers to a great degree. Mentally inert because of his personal problems, both real and imagined, the sergeant typifies the examples of apathy and preoccupation that appear as the true causes in many police officer deaths—if we truthfully reconstruct each case.

Officer Baker helped set it up too. Baker's thoughts strayed momentarily, and he paid a crippling price for a few moments of inattention. Carl, even David, helped set it up. Properly responding to the call was their responsibility. Responsibility does not cease upon arrival. Both assumed all was under control because, when they stopped in front of the bank two officers were already there. They also believed the call to be another false alarm. The assumptions caused them to relax too soon. Relaxing too soon is one of the deadly errors mentioned in the first chapter. Carl and David did not remain alert long enough to be sure that any chance of danger had been checked out and eliminated. Their errors cost them their lives. To attempt to establish the cost to their families is an impossible task.

And the department set them up. Administrative procrastination over a procedural change had led to a mental block among patrol officers regarding silent alarm calls.

This case is one of the classic tragedies. It is not pleasant to recall, much less relate, the details of the incident. It is not a popular subject discussed by police officers during a coffee break. Some officers I know strongly resent any implication that the officers in this case were in any way to blame. Their understandably bitter feelings towards the murderers have completely shut out any possible acknowledgement of the errors committed by the four officers. But we cannot afford to disregard unpleasant facts when police officers are murdered in the line of duty. Difficult as it is, we must accept the fact that many, too many, law enforcement officers who die in the field have made mistakes. Perhaps not intentionally, but errors nevertheless. An awareness of the errors and constant alertness will, without doubt, greatly increase the police officer's chances for survival on the street.

sleepy sam

4

sleepy sam

4

During the SLEEPY, or ASLEEP lecture presentations of "Survival On The Street" I have many times heard a muted chuckle and observed knowing smiles from my police officer audience. I wonder: are they thinking "hell's bells, everybody does it once in awhile. A little nap now and then on a slow night never hurt anyone."?

This is the story of Sam Reid, policeman. A 26 year veteran policeman. Sam was a sleeper too, and he never got hurt. Or did he?

The sergeant paused as the familiar straggler entered the big room.

"Well what's the excuse this time Sam?"

"Sorry Sarge, left the house a little late I guess."

Sam Reid was a big man. It had been said that during the war, Reid, an Air Force Corporal, was unfondly referred to as "Corpulent" Reid by his subordinates. How he'd managed to pass his physical when he came on the job was a department mystery. He sat down heavily in the front row and finished buttoning his shirt, which still hung outside his pants, and picked up the black necktie draped over the butt of the revolver that swung at his side in a worn leather holster. He smiled and said, "I had to finish the count for the ticket sales. Lieutenant's orders, you know. He wants our shift and this division to be the highest in the . . ."

"O.K., O.K., Sam, I know," said the sergeant impatiently. "Now let's finish roll call." The sergeant picked up the clipboard from the desk and quickly read off the names.

"Burton."

"Here."

"Clifford."

"Yup."

He looked up at his men and dealt the assignments: "Burton, Clifford, car One Twenty One. Make an area check in the vicinity of 12th and Gladstone. People complaining of refrigerator trucks parking in the neighborhood and leaving their motors running. Nobody gets any sleep." The two officers nodded and made a notation at the bottom of their hot sheet.

"Dewey."

"Here sir."

The sergeant looked up again. Dewey's young face was easy to
spot in the familiar group of 18 men. Fresh out of the academy,
unspoiled and eager to go. Dewey looked sharp too. An example
of the bright youngsters the department was looking for these
days. And, thought the sergeant, I'm all for it. Makes my job
easier; I'd like to have a dozen more Deweys. Just too bad they
have to mix with a few of these old bastards still hanging around.
He glanced at the front row and slammed his fist on the table.

"Damn it, Sam wake up! I don't care if you are our rep. You got
eight hours to go yet until seven in the morning. Don't fall asleep
on me during roll call."

"Sorry Sarge." Reid picked up his tie that had slipped to the
floor and placed it around his collar. "It was a rough day at the
office, really." He turned and grinned at the group behind him.

"We all feel for you Sam," responded the sergeant. "You're
working car One Eleven with Dewey. He's a new man and the
lieutenant has assigned him to you for field training."

"Sure Sarge, I'll take good care of him. Like I always do."

The sergeant stood up. "Let's go to work. Remember, start
writing more F.I.'s. Real ones. Not off the headstones in the
cemetery. What used to be done in the good old days doesn't go
anymore."

As the men rose and began to file out of the room, an enormous

65

belch erupted from within officer Sam Reid.

"Jesus," said a voice in the rear of the group, "Was that a king size belch or a queen size fart?"

"Doesn't matter," said another, "If that was Sam Reid it'll smell the same no matter which end it came out of." Then leaning closer to his partner, he continued, "That poor kid. The glory instilled at the academy is going to be blown to hell after working a few nights with old Sam."

"Yeah, ol' buddy, but remember all of us had to be baptized by foul Sam, part of the initiation in the Fourth Patrol Division. But maybe it won't be so bad on the new guy. He's working the grave-yard shift and Sam won't be able to screw him up too bad—he'll be sleeping most of the time."

"Yeah," laughed the other officer, "But his snoring can sure be embarrassing if you have to stop for a red light at a crowded intersection."

Officer Ken Dewey waited patiently for his partner in the park-ing lot next to the old redstone police building. He'd completed the inspection check on car One Eleven and all was in good order. Dewey was nervous and apprehensive but he eagerly looked forward to his first night on patrol. The police academy had been great, even better than he'd expected. And to top it off, he'd been elected class president. Melinda, his obviously preg-nant young wife, had been so proud. He was lucky, he thought; he noticed that many of the wives of his classmates were visibly apprehensive about their husbands' occupation. But not Melinda. Three months before she'd watched him during grad-uation exercises when he'd received his A.A. degree at Central Community College. Since then he had registered, and was ready to start at, State University in the fall. In three or four years he'd have his degree. Everything was going according to plan. Tonight he'd finally be doing what he'd wanted to do for years. "To Serve and To Protect" was the department's motto, and Ken Dewey fully intended to do just that.

Dewey saw Sam Reid come out of the door marked "Police Personnel Only" and amble slowly towards him. *Twenty six years on the job,* Dewey marvelled. *Sam had already been a policeman for three years when I was born! I guess he's seen just about everything. I wonder what kind of a man he is?*

Sam Reid, 26 year patrol veteran elicited various descriptions from the many persons who had known or had worked with him.

His partner of five years, now retired had said:

"Sam was a good partner. Sensible. Not a hero type, but that was fine with me. I lived to retire after 25 years and Sam is still alive and healthy."

And his sergeant:

"Sam is really an outgoing guy. He needs attention and wants very much to be liked by everybody. I know he's working over the limit allowed on that off-duty security job, but he'll retire soon anyway and do that full-time. Basically, Sam is lazy. I think he has been since I've known him, going on ten years I guess. The last few years he's definitely been getting worse. I wouldn't let him near the rookies we get from the academy, but the lieutenant is the boss on the shift and says that's what he wants Sam to do, break in the new cops. I guess the lieutenant ought to know Sam better than I do. They went through the academy over 26 years ago."

Sam's lieutenant called him:

"A good ol' boy. Maybe not a hard charger anymore, maybe never was. But after all those years a man's earned the right to an assignment he wants. It's seniority that counts, ask any old-timer. Sam's done a lot for the division too. He leads the whole department in ticket sales for the police show every year. He gets us our Christmas turkeys at a real good price and volunteers every year to hustle up the food for the division picnic. He asked to work the graveyard shift and be able to train the rookies. If that's what he wants, that's what I'll let him do. Only thing that bothers me is our new Captain. He seems interested in Sam and how he's doing. Why, I don't know. New Captains are usually a pain in the ass for awhile anyway. This one could be worse, he's only got 16 years on the job and is Captain already."

The Captain observed that:

"After three months at Fourth Patrol Division I think I have Sam Reid properly evaluated: he is a lazy incompetent. I can't believe he was ever a good policeman. He is a classic example of one year of experience completed 26 times. He is living only for the day he can retire and be assured his new job will be easier than the way he now works for the department. When he does retire the department will take another progressive step forward. Next week I am going to tell the lieutenant that I want him transferred to the day shift, so he can be watched and made to produce. He will definitely not be used from then on as a field training officer for the new men we receive from the academy."

Ken Dewey stood at the front of the car as Sam Reid approached.

"Who do you want to drive first tonight sir?"

Reid walked by his young partner without stopping. "You drive kid—all night." He opened the passenger door and seated himself. "It's the only way you're going to learn where the streets are. Let's get going. Pull out of the lot and take a right on First Street."

Officer Dewey was pleased; he'd wanted to drive. He started the car and drove out of the lot into a light flow of traffic. Several minutes and a few blocks later Reid lit a cigarette and asked Dewey if he knew the beat boundaries. "Yes sir," came the prompt reply.

Reid dragged happily on his cigarette. Good deal, he thought. This one has been well trained and is still respectful. "O.K. kid, you just keep driving. Stay inside our beat. I'm going to take a little nap. If anything happens you wake me up. Understand?"

Dewey tried not to look as startled as he felt. He nodded to indicate an understanding, not necessarily acceptance, of this obvious violation of department policy.

"One thing more," said Reid, putting out his cigarette, "if you get a Code 3 call, for chrissake wake me up before you turn on the frigging siren. Last guy I had did that and I just about crapped in my pants. I think the smart ass did it on purpose, but don't you try it."

Dewey nodded again concealing his disappointment as Reid tipped his hat forward and slumped down in the seat. A minute later Dewey realized that for all practical purposes he was completely alone in a patrol car on his very first night of duty.

By 0200 hours car One Eleven had received a family disturbance call and made two traffic stops after Ken Dewey had observed two errant motorists before they had seen him. Each time Dewey had awakened Reid, he was chewed out for unnecessarily disturbing his older partner's nap. The family quarrel had been easily patched up and the motorists had been chagrined and apologetic.

"Dammit kid," growled Reid when Dewey woke him up for the third time, "learn to handle these things yourself. Someday you'll be working alone in a car on the day shift in a no-problem beat. Then who the hell is going to help you figure these things out? Now let me finish my nap."

At 0315 hours car One Eleven got a Code 2 fight call. Officer Dewey looked at his partner. It was obvious by now that Reid's naps were close to a form of hibernation. But he woke him immediately and advised him of the call.

Reid growled like a sleepy old bear. "You could've got there first you know, before you woke me up. Most fights are over before we can arrive anyway. But I guess you haven't learned that yet. Now for chrissakes slow down, let them fight it out. Take it easy and they might even be gone when we get there. Next time, see if you can work out one of these things on your own."

At 0435 hours Officer Reid was jolted out of his deep sleep by three quick and loud blasts. The last awakened him to reality: gunfire that had to be a shotgun. Reid looked to his left and screamed, "What the Hell you got us into now?" before he realized his young partner was not in the patrol car with him. As Reid opened the door a car twenty feet in front of him roared away with tires screeching. Then in the glare of the headlights, he saw Dewey lying face down and motionless in the street. Reid ran to where his young partner lay and turned him over. He gasped as he saw the terrible wound and the chalk white face. Then feeling the warm and sticky fluid, he pulled his hand back from a gaping hole in Dewey's chest. Reid stood up and sucked in air to keep his legs steady under him. Good God, he thought,

70

if he isn't already dead he's bleeding to death. He stumbled back to the car, picked up the microphone, pushed the button, took several deep breaths and trying hard to keep from choking up, spoke into the microphone.

"Car One Eleven—shots fired—my partner has been hit—bad I think. Send an ambulance. Officers need help."

The dispatcher responded instantly and sharply. "All units on all frequencies stand by—a shooting and officers need help. Car One Eleven—your location?"

Then Sam Reid froze. Fear gripped him, the gnawing fear that he had carefully avoided for 26 years now engulfed him and was tightening in his chest so that he could hardly breathe. Frantically he looked up and down the quiet alley he was standing in—where his young partner lay bleeding to death. There were no familiar landmarks. Sam Reid had no idea of his location.

"Car One Eleven, Car One Eleven, come in with your location. Come in with your location."

No, Sam Reid didn't get hurt—not physically hurt. But 21 days after the shooting and 18 days after Ken Dewey's funeral Sam Reid suddenly retired. No one really knew if it was because of the large bronze framed picture of Ken Dewey that was placed in the entry way of the old police station just two days before Sam retired. Or maybe it was because nobody talked to Sam anymore, not for three weeks—not even to say hello.

Like they say: "Hell's bells, a little nap on a slow night never hurt anyone."

dark nights, dark deeds

dark nights, dark deeds

5

"Still raining, Clint?" asked the man at the desk as he hung up the phone.

"Yeh, a little harder than when we came in."

Clinton Ramsey sipped slowly from a big coffee mug. Then he turned and sat down next to the large table. "What was that call all about?"

The man at the desk got up and walked to the large window. He struck a match, held it close, and pulled on the pipe. "The sergeant downstairs in patrol wants to know if anyone here wants to get into a study group for the sergeant's and lieutenant's exams next month. I suppose you'll be taking it, huh?"

"Why not? Nothing to lose. Either way I'm ahead. Make it and get a raise, flunk it and I stay here. Can't beat that. What about you, Charley Jones? You would be one of the best sergeants in the business if you'd just take that damn written. I know you'd get a top oral."

"Crap on that," said Detective Charles Jones. "You know what the policy is: get a promotion and out you go. Transferred to another division, probably back to patrol. Why give up the best job in the department, night watch, Major Crimes Division? All the hot calls, all the action, and none of the drudgery and pressure of the day watch teams who have to follow up and figure out whodunnit, or walking a beat for patrol in this lousy rain."

"Jesus, Charley, I think you've been watching those goofy TV cop shows too much. Patrol's not that bad, and you know damn well that with your reputation, you'd get back in Major Crimes in a year or two."

The phone rang. Ramsey reached across the table and raised the receiver. He swung his legs up, leaned back and put his feet on the old oak table top.

"Major Crimes, Ramsey."

"Do I talk to you about a murder?" the voice at the other end said.

"Sure, how can I help you?"

"You're a lot nicer than that other cop."

"Who's that?"

"The one that answered the phone first."

"Oh, well he works another part of the department," said Ramsey. "He's supposed to transfer calls; maybe he's bored with his job. Now, what's this about a murder?"

"Can you murder an animal, a dog?"

"No, not according to the law. Murder means killing another person. So you could kill a dog, but it's not a murder. What's your name?"

"Why?"

"I'd just like to know. I told you mine, I'm Sergeant Ramsey."

"I'd rather not—will you still talk with me?"

"Sure I will. Can you tell me where you live?"

"No, the address isn't important right now. It will be later though."

The officer sat up, put his feet under the table. He looked up at his partner who furrowed his brows and returned a quizzical look.

"Okay, how come you wanted to know about murdering a dog? Is there a reason you asked me?"

"Yes, I just hung Snow."

"Snow?"

"Yes. Snow is my dog. He was so beautiful too. Pure white."

"You hung your dog, a real dog?"

Ramsey looked at his partner, raised his right hand and made a circling motion, index finger extended, around his right ear. Then he pointed at the phone and held up two fingers.

Detective Jones sat down quickly, put his pipe in a large pottery ash tray, pushed the extension 212 button and carefully picked up the phone. He nodded to the detective engaged in the conversation and began to make short quick notes with a pencil on the legal pad in front of him.

"Why would you want to hang a dog?"

"For practice. I'm going to have to hang myself later this evening."

"Hey, I'm getting all mixed up. You're going too fast for me. Can you start over? Back up and start over."

Detective Charley Jones carefully placed his phone receiver on the pad, then got up and walked to another table at the far end of the room. He dialed a three digit number, waited, then spoke into the phone.

"Wayne, this is Charley Jones down in Major Crimes. Ramsey has a crazy on extension 212 that's going to hang himself. See if you can do a trace. If you get it call us back. Call on extension 215, I'll answer and get patrol rolling to bust in on him . . . Yeh, right, thanks."

Detective Jones hung up, then returned to his desk, picked up the phone and continued to make notes as he listened to the conversation between Ramsey and the stranger.

"Sure, I'll tell you why. It's all very simple. My girlfriend, my ex-girlfriend, is coming over in about a half hour to give me her ring back. The engagement ring. She's jilted me. She even laughed about it and called me a creep. She thinks she can insult me and get away with it, but she'll get a nice surprise when she gets here. That's why I hung Snow; I did it for practice. When Val gets here, she'll join Snow. There's no point in spending my life in

78

jail, so I'll join them. When you find us, you'll see the three of us hanging there side by side Sergeant, and I'm telling you now so you won't think you have a mystery to solve."

The two detectives glanced at each other. Jones muttered silently as he listened, "Unbelievable. You'd think after 15 years you have seen and heard it all—now we get a loony psycho who's killed his dog for practice before he commits a murder-suicide."

"You're kidding," said Ramsey, "What's the point? No female's worth all that."

"It's important to me. I've made up my mind."

"What's Val's last name?"

"Won't tell."

"How are we going to find you? You're going to have to tell me where you live."

"No, I won't tell you where I live. I have to finish my plan first. But I realize what kind of mess this room will be in if you don't find all of us by tomorrow. So I'll give you a clue so you can find me quicker, but it will take you long enough so you won't be able to stop me. I live by the airport."

"That wouldn't help Sherlock Holmes find you. Thousands of people live by the airport."

(Laughing) "I know."

"You got a window in your house?"

"Yes, a big one."

"What do you see out of it?"

"I told you, the airport. I can see airplanes landing, and taking off."

"You can see them landing on the runway?"

"Sure."

"That helps a little. Give me another clue. If you go over to your window you can see a plane coming in for a landing, right?"

"Right."

"And it's coming in from the left side of your window, if the plane takes off it goes up and out the right side of your window, correct?"

"Right, but how can that be a clue? They fly in and out that way all the time."

"I admit it's not much of a clue, how about something else?"

Ramsey wrote quickly on a pad, then signaled his partner. Jones got up, walked to his partner's table, picked up the note and hurried to the phone at the far side of the room. He sat down and dialed a number.

"Airport patrol? This is Charley Jones in Major Crimes. Take some notes fast, this is an emergency. We gotta crazy on the phone. Says he's going to murder his girlfriend, who's supposed to show up at his pad in about 20-30 minutes, then he's going to hang himself . . . right . . . Okay, this guy is playing games about where he's located, but we're making a guess. We think we've got a fix on him from what he's said. No, we don't know his name . . . he won't give any kind of name, but he says he can look out his window and see the planes land and take off, and from his left to his right as he watches them . . . Right. It has to be Aloha Towers, the only other place, the Conners Condominiums, is on the south side of the field. Anyone there would see planes coming in right to left. And he says he has a pure white dog named Snow. Get a team together and go to the Aloha Towers. See if anyone there can help you. Maybe with luck the manager would know of a young male adult living in the south side of the building that keeps a white dog named Snow. Managers usually keep track of such things. If there is, you've got to take a chance and go in on him . . . Right, call us back. We'll try to keep him on the line. Good luck."

Detective Jones returned to his seat and picked up the phone. He dropped a note on his partner's desk as he walked by.

Ramsey picked up the note and read:

Airport patrol will check it out, stand by for a kicked in front door, I hope.

He looked at Jones, nodded, then spoke into the phone again. "Now, you know there's a better way. You going to do this all for one little dolly that jokered you? There's lots and lots of girls around town you know, all kinds, shapes, sizes and capabilities."

"I know, but nobody can put me down like she did. She's got to pay."

"There's a better way. Want to hear it?"

"I don't know. I think I'm giving you too much time anyway."

"How can I stop you as long as I'm on the phone? There's no

way, no possible way I can get to you. I don't even know your name."

"You sure?"

"Of course. I'm sitting here at police headquarters 10 miles from the airport. I don't even know who or where you are. How could I get to you?'

"Okay, I guess you can't. What's the better way?"

"Good, I'll tell you. There's a better way to punish her. You said she jilted you, why don't you jilt her?"

"Exactly what I'm going to do, with a knife and a rope."

"No man, not that way. Call her up and tell her she's no good. Not good enough for you."

For several minutes Ramsey kept the conversation going. Then suddenly he heard a loud splintering crash, a scream and loud voices on the other end of the line. "Hold it buddy boy, just hold it, everything will be okay, calm down, calm down, this won't hurt a bit."

Then, "Bastards, bastards, liar, lying bastards."

Ramsey heard the phone scrape on a solid surface.

"Anyone there?"

"Yeh, Ramsey, Major Crimes. Who's this?"

"Oh, hi Sarge. This is Smitty, airport detail. We got your crazy. His name is Victor Rogers, living in room 1432, fourteenth floor of the Aloha Towers. He's . . . son of a bitch, we just opened the closet door and found Snow. What a beautiful dog, a pure white Samoyed, hung up . . . dead. That frigging screwball, you should've let him hang himself."

"Yeh, but he was going to kill his girlfriend first. She's due there in about a half hour."

"Oh, well, I guess that's different. We'll leave her a note. And, Sarge, . . ."

"Yes?"

"Crazy Victor here says he has a message for you. He says tell Sergeant Ramsey he's a fucking liar. You said you wouldn't be able to stop him."

"I got a message for Victor. Tell him that was no lie, that's an investigative technique."

"I'll tell him, Sarge. Thanks."

As Ramsey and Jones replace the receivers in front of them, another phone rang.

"Oh, yeh, Wayne . . . Right. The Aloha Towers, room 1432. You had it right. We got lucky and just had airport detail bust the guy. Tell the phone company thanks, they did a good job, a quick job. Adios."

"Man, what a crazy." Jones shook his head, then re-lighted his pipe. "You did a hell of a job on that Clint. That calls for a drink. I'll buy." Ramsey laughed as his partner walked to the coffee machine and inserted two dimes.

Jones walked back carrying the two steaming cups. "What did I tell you? Where in the department can you get such action?" Charley Jones sat down and continued. "Who else in the department could get to do what we just did?"

"A patrol sergeant and his team made the bust, don't forget that."

"Yeh, but now they have to babysit that nut until some shrink decides he's safe enough to let loose. Then when he is turned loose in a couple days, he'll be a problem for patrol again, wait and see."

The phone rang. Clint Ramsey picked it up and listened. He made brief notes, then said, "Right, we're on the way. See you there, Lieutenant." He turned to his partner, "Our turn to roll. I'll fill you in on the way down." Both men got up. Jones opened a desk drawer and picked up an oversized red enameled key ring.

Ramsey briefed his partner on the information just received as they hurried down the hall and then down the elevator to the basement of the police building.

"The old Bijou, that little neighborhood movie house at 13th and Main." Jones nodded as Ramsey continued. "Guy went in and shot up the place. Apparently he's a boyfriend, ex-boyfriend sounds like, of the girl in the ticket booth. She's dead. The night manager tried to be a hero and got shot too. Patrol's there waiting for us. The crime scene techs are on the way."

"It's our night for crazys and lovers quarrels," said Jones without emotion as he started the car.

"Let's roll, code 3," said Ramsey.

"Patrol's already there."

"Yeh," said the Sergeant. "But the shooter's still loose and we're going to be the guys who have to run him down."

Jones nodded, flicked two switches on the dashboard and pressed the horn ring.

Four minutes later they were half a block from the scene in heavy traffic. The curious drivers ahead of them all but refused to move through the intersection while they stared at the activity on the southwest corner.

Four patrol units and a stubbornly curious crowd of pedestrians forced the two detectives and the patrol lieutenant, trailing in his blue and white Dodge, to double park across the street from the little theater. As the three men stepped out into the street, an ambulance left, twin sirens blaring.

The shooting, according to the young patrol sergeant who met them, happened in the foyer of the theater. "Suspect is Hoyt, Roger," the Sergeant read from his field notebook. "Male, Cauc, 36, 5'8", 190, brown and brown. Five-day growth of beard. Wearing dark slacks, black raincoat, dark hat."

"He's well camouflaged for a night like this," grumped Jones. "I wonder if he dressed that way on purpose?"

"Description out?" asked the patrol lieutenant.

"Yes sir," said the Sergeant. "Hansen put it out. He was here first. Soon as he made sure the suspect was gone and an ambulance was coming, he put out the description."

"Okay, Sarge," asked Ramsey, "What's the rest of it, what happened?"

"We have two wits. One is the girlfriend of the deceased."

The men glanced momentarily at the body next to a wall under a red-stained white sheet left by the ambulance crew. The Sergeant paused, then continued. "The other is the night manager. The manager is in bad shape. Gut shot, looked like to me."

"Where are your witnesses?" asked Ramsey.

"They all went in the ambulance."

"Dammit to hell," said Jones. "How come? We need to talk to them."

The uniformed lieutenant looked at his patrol sergeant and frowned.

The sergeant nodded. "I think we got enough for you. We're working on the rest." He looked at the notes held in his hand. "Mrs. Wagner, the manager's wife, wanted to be with her husband. No way we could stop her from getting in that ambulance; besides, she didn't see the shooting or the suspect. The other witness is Sarah Young, 19 years. She saw the shooting and knows and can identify the suspect. She told us the story. Then some dummy that works here part-time started screaming, 'Janie's been killed, Janie's been killed.' Sarah didn't know her friend was dead. She passed out cold. When she came to, she was hysterical. We had to put her in the ambulance. Lucky we got her story before she heard the bad news."

The patrol lieutenant relaxed and smiled as Detective Jones spoke. "Okay, Sarge, sorry I growled at you. Your guys did a hell of a good job all around. Now let's get the rest of it so we can try to pick up this crazy."

"Okay," the sergeant continued to read from his field notebook.

"You have his description. He lives at 7454 South Palmer Drive. No phone. At least his family lives there. He has a wife and three kids. He drives a '71 Mustang, silver grey, license, 6 Edward Henry, 240. Apparently he has been stepping out on his old lady and shacking up with the victim. Her name is Jane West. Sarah, our witness, told us Jane had mentioned Hoyt. Said he was a wealthy businessman that had fallen in love with her. Gave her the usual baloney. He was going to divorce his wife and marry her. That was a couple of months ago. Three days ago Janie told Sarah it was all off. Roger was some kind of a beast, and a liar. He didn't have lots of money. He liked to do bad things that hurt when they did their thing. Besides, Janie had found a new nice young boyfriend her own age who had a new Jag and money to burn."

"Got his name?" asked Ramsey. "He could be next."

"Not yet, but we're checking."

"Okay, go ahead."

The sergeant nodded and continued. "Tonight at about 2330 hours the show was shutting down for the night. Just employees aboard. Hoyt, the suspect, tapped on the foyer door. The part-time kid had seen him before with Janie and didn't know about the breakup so she let him in. Sarah, our witness, came out just in time to see Hoyt pointing a gun at Janie and yell, "You dirty cheating little bitch, you're going to be the first to die tonight."

"Oh, oh," interrupted Jones, "You were right, Clint." The patrol sergeant paused, then continued to read from his notes.

"The suspect pulled the trigger about four times. Looks like he used a .38, a revolver. No ejects. We are pretty sure she got hit at least four times. We got one slug located under a drape."

"Good," Ramsey and Jones both nodded as the sergeant continued.

"When the shooting started, Sarah turned and ran back into the office. That's where we found her when we arrived. When she ran back into the office, the manager, who had heard the shots, ran out of his office into the foyer. I guess that's when he caught his. He took one in the belly and one over the knee."

The sergeant returned his notebook to his shirt pocket and pointed to a room marked "Manager's Office." "I've a man in the office running a record check on our suspect and trying to locate the victim's new boyfriend. I also asked the officer who rode in the ambulance to call me here if and when he has anything to report."

The four men walked by the young victim as a photo lab crew removed the sheet and began to adjust their cameras.

Ramsey turned toward the young patrol sergeant. "Sergeant, you did a real nice job down here tonight. Saved us a lot of time. It should make it easier to pick up our shooter. Why don't you come and see us some afternoon in Major Crimes Division? We need a couple more good men, and the captain said yesterday we had an opening coming up."

"You just keep your cotton pickers off him Ramsey," said the big patrol lieutenant. "I need good men just as much as you do."

Ramsey laughed. "You outrank me lieutenant, so I'll shut up. But I bet our captain tries to do something about it."

"Always the way," said the lieutenant shaking his head. "Get a good man trained for the street and the dicks pick him off."

As the men entered the small theater office, the uniformed officer hung up the phone and handed a sheet of paper to his sergeant. "He's got a record all right, Sarge, and look at that third entry." The four men read the officer's writing together.

"Wouldn't you know," said Jones. "Two CCW's, a DUI, a resisting, and, Jesus, two mental health holds in the last three years."

"They didn't hold him long enough," said Ramsey.

"What else is new?" grumbled the lieutenant.

"Anything on that boyfriend?"

"No sir," said the officer seated next to the phone, "not yet." The phone rang and he picked it up. "Hello, yes this is Fisher." He listened, looked up and said, "Just a minute, Sergeant Ramsey of Major Crimes is here, you better tell him." He handed the phone to the detective.

"This is Ramsey, go ahead." He listened then said, "Okay, we'll take care of it. Will he make it or not? What's the doc think?" Then he put down the phone and turned to the policeman standing next to him.

"Bad news, the night manager is very critical, they're not sure they can save him. When they were rolling him into surgery, your man," he nodded to the patrol sergeant, "noticed he had come to and was trying to say something.

"As they walked along, he bent down and the manager whispered in the officer's ear. After Hoyt shot him, he walked up to him and pulled the trigger again, twice. The gun didn't fire. I guess that confirms that it was a revolver, he'd used up all six. Then Hoyt kicked the guy and said, 'Two more to go, her boyfriend and my wife. Nobody screws me around.' Then Hoyt ran out the front door."

"Damn," said Jones, "We got to get him quick. He's going to knock off a guy we can't even ID yet, then kill his wife."

"Sounds that way," said Ramsey. "And she's got three kids at home with her."

"What a fine gentleman he must be," grumbled the lieutenant.

"He kills his shack job because she was cheating on him, and now he wants to kill his wife who stays home minding the kids while he's out screwing around. We got a real crazy to find."

"Yeh," nodded Jones. "The woods are full of them tonight."

"Okay, here's what we do. My partner and I will head out to Hoyt's house to watch for him there. Sarge, you keep trying to locate this unknown boyfriend of the victim. If you locate him, you know what to do and who to call. We're going to cut out. We'll get a copy of the preliminary investigation report in the morning."

"Right, good luck."

The two detectives waved to the uniformed officers as they walked out of the office and passed the body of the victim, now being attended to by a coroner's deputy. As they entered their car, Ramsey looked up, "Rain's let up a bit, but it's sure dark out tonight."

"Dark night, dark deeds," mumbled Jones as he started the car. The two detectives drove south on a now almost deserted main street.

The neighborhood in the 7400 block of South Palmer Drive was about as unique as the typical American upper middle-class suburban neighborhood in hundreds of metropolitan areas across the United States. By 0100 hours, one and one-half hours after the fatal shooting at the movie house, the neighborhood surrounding 7454 South Palmer Drive had been checked out by Detectives Ramsey and Jones. They noted the lights were on at 7454, but there was no apparent activity. Surely, if Hoyt had returned home, many lights would have been on in quite a few houses, particularly those next to 7454.

There was no sign of the silver grey Mustang near or within several blocks of the house. The garage door of the home had been left open but the garage was empty. The green Chevrolet parked in the driveway had been noted and the license number checked for want and registration. A few minutes later, the police dispatcher had advised Ramsey and Jones that there was no want on the car and that it was registered to a Thomas Blaney with an address in a suburb on the west side of the river that bordered the city.

"Let's go have a talk with her. If she doesn't already know, somebody has to tell her. She has to be warned anyway."

"Right," said Jones. He slowed and stopped the police car at the curb in front of the house.

The officers walked side by side, across the wet grass of the parkway, across the sidewalk, past the shoulder high and well-trimmed Juniper bushes that bordered the lawn, and up the cement walk leading to the front door. The lights were on, all shades were drawn, and they could hear the murmur of low voices from within. They drew their weapons. Jones stood on one side as Ramsey leaned over from the other and pressed the doorbell.

"Who's there?" It was a man's voice, loud but obviously anxious. Both officers tensed. Crouching down and moving further back from the door, Ramsey called out loudly, "Police officers, we want to talk with Mrs. Hoyt."

"Just a minute," said the voice from within. The men outside then heard a woman's voice. "That's not Roger, I know his voice."

"How do we know you're the police?"

Ramsey removed a black leather wallet from his pocket. Placing it against a door window pane, he shouted, "I'm Sergeant Ramsey. I'm holding my badge and ID card against the door window. Read it, then please open up, I must talk to you."

A few seconds later the door opened and a man looked out. "There's two of us," Ramsey replied quickly. "My partner and I, we're police detectives." Both men held out their badges.

"Okay, we had to make sure it wasn't Roger. Come on in, I want to close the door." The two officers entered the room and were led to the lighted kitchen area. Mrs. Hoyt, eyes red and swollen, was pouring a cup of coffee with an unsteady hand.

"I'm Thomas Blaney. I'm Hilda's brother. We know what happened. I'm trying to get her out of here to come and stay with us, but she won't leave. The kids don't know. They're asleep in the bedroom. Will you try to convince her to get out of here?"

"Yes," said Ramsey. "It would be best, Mrs. Hoyt. Won't you go with your brother? We'll stand by while you leave."

"You can't stand by me forever," she replied without looking up. "He'll find me and kill me and the kids too. Dear God, he's completely lost his mind. We saw it coming years ago but the doctors just passed it off as hypertension. He should've been committed a year ago. I don't know what to do, but I know I won't leave my house. I feel more safe here than anywhere else. At least I know this place."

For almost ten more minutes, Thomas Blaney tried to convince his sister that she should leave her home, at least temporarily. Then, realizing the futility of his argument, Mr. Blaney said he would stay with his sister, at least for the rest of the night. Mrs. Hoyt consented.

Before leaving, the two officers asked that they be called if any member of the family heard from Mr. Hoyt, and advised that the police emergency number be called if for any reason they believed the fugitive was in the vicinity. They would also see to it that a watch would be placed on the house for the rest of the night. They, or other detectives, would check with Mrs. Hoyt again in the morning.

The detectives then walked from the kitchen to the front door, opened it, stepped out on the front porch, and into the dark night. As they walked toward their car, they talked.

"Wonder where he is?" asked Jones pulling his coat around him.

"Probably looking for that kid, the boyfriend."

"Well, you did a good job of locating one crazy earlier tonight

Clint, that nut who hung his dog. I hope you can come up with some ideas on this one."

Ramsey nodded in the dark. "I think we will. Hoyt shouldn't be too hard to find. No psycho hides himself very well. He'll give himself away by doing something crazy."

As the two officers walked by the juniper bushes bordering the sidewalk, a man in a dark coat and hat stepped forward and raised the gun in his hand. He fired. One shot, then a second.

Detective Sergeant Clint Ramsey saw, for only a split second, the blinding light. The sound of the shot was gone almost instantaneously as the bullet entered his right temple and tore through his brain. He was dead when he collapsed and fell on the sidewalk.

Detective Charley Jones had only a moment to turn and begin the reflex action of throwing back his coat to reach for his gun. While turning to meet his attacker, he saw the second flash and heard the shot at the same instant he felt the searing burn on the right side of his chest. Detective Jones, driven backwards by the force of the bullet, fell into the juniper bushes that had provided concealment for the killer. Looking up, the officer was able to see the man in the dark coat sprint for the house. He heard the man scream, "Tonight's the end for all of us, the end, the end!"

Detective Jones, gun in hand, rolled with considerable difficulty into the position he had taken many times at the department PPC. He fired three quick shots. As if in slow motion, Detective Jones watched the man stagger, turn, drop his gun, then fall forward on the steps in front of his home.

The format of this incident, the story of the last night on duty and the murder of Detective Sergeant Clinton Ramsey and the shooting of his partner Detective Charles Jones, was presented in this manner to emphasize a very important, perhaps the most important point in this book.

The two detectives, Ramsey and Jones, were fine men. Not fine because they were officers, but fine because they were experienced, hard working, dedicated, and intelligent. Police officers who die are not necessarily unintelligent, lazy clods. The great tragedy is that some of the very best have died unnecessarily.

Clint Ramsey was one of the best, and so was his partner. There appears to be no logical reason why two experienced detectives would walk into an ambush the morning they were working the Hoyt case. Both men were sharp. They knew each other and they knew their job. They had carefully checked the neighborhood for the suspect before they went to his house. Why, then, the fatal slip when they left the house? Perhaps it did not seem likely that the killer would stay in the vicinity after seeing the police car in front of the house. Perhaps, considering the circumstances, they should have recovered their diminished night vision before walking from the lighted house into the very dark night. Not remaining constantly alert, however, for just a few seconds at the wrong time, was the cause, the "why" a fine officer died and the other received a permanent disabling injury.

It is because they are human that police officers make fatal errors. They will work hard for long hours at a job with great stress. They save lives, protect the innocent, and even those not so innocent. Then on occasion, they commit an error. They get preoccupied. They relax. An act of great, but unnecessary courage is diluted with carelessness; or after many years, like most people, they get apathetic. For police officers, these are fatal and deadly errors. For police officers, remaining constantly alert is not only a way of life, it is a necessity for survival on the street.

the gun that wouldn't shoot

the gun that wouldn't shoot 6

I believe it necessary to discuss the care and use of the police officer's gun and his "office," the patrol car he is assigned to and must sit in for an average of five to eight hours a day. Both the weapon and the car are an important, but many times forgotten, aspect of police officer survival on the street.

Many excellent articles and books have been written about firearms training and the proper use and care of the police service revolver and automatic weapons. Most departments, at least those with a degree of pride and responsible governmental support, will provide training enabling their police officers to become proficient in firearms use, and perhaps more importantly, taught when and when not to shoot.

Unfortunately, little has been written about the importance of providing the field officer with a vehicle that is both efficient and safe. And, too few departments provide high speed driving safety training for their police officers. Fewer yet rely on comprehensive road tests to establish acceptable performance specifications prior to letting out bids for their police vehicles.

Most certainly, the police officer has a responsibility. He must, without fail:

1. Keep his service weapon in excellent condition.

2. Wear the weapon properly. Too many officers wear their guns in positions that have been identified as:

   a). "BB" (Ball Buster). The gun is slung low just to the right or left of the belt buckle.

   b). "Suicide." The gun is in a cross-draw holster, grip extended forward. This greatly assists the psychopath who is resisting custody in disarming the officer. I recently saw an officer whose gun and grip were thrust forward proudly. That officer would have never been allowed to follow anybody in a close order drill.

3. Become proficient in the use of firearms. Monthly qualifications at an established firearms range should be the goal of the department and the officer. The department that fails to provide this training for its officers is shirking its responsibility. And so is the officer who does not find time to practice on his own if he or she is not provided with this training by the employer. (When that unexpected close range fire-fight starts, there is no time to stop and clean the gun to make sure it will fire, and no one will aim it for you.)

4. Meticulously check the patrol vehicle and all accessories prior to beginning a tour of duty. Mechanical problems should be reported and a preventive maintenance system should provide a method to correct problems as soon as possible.

Numbers 1 and 3 above—keeping the service weapon in excellent condition and proficiency with the weapon—require individual effort by the police officer. Either one by itself is worthless; the absence of both could have disastrous results.

I would like to believe that every police officer sincerely hopes he will never have to fire his gun at a person for any reason. But as long as violent crimes are committed against the public and the police by persons using deadly force, then the police must be properly trained, equipped and ready to use deadly force when lawful and necessary. It would seem unlikely that a police officer would carry a gun just for show or because in America, it is traditional to do so. Unfortunately, this incredible situation has occurred, but luckily, such cases are rare.

This is the story of one of those instances. I call it, "The Gun That Wouldn't Shoot."

Jeff Mitchell coughed and cracked the window even though it was cold outside. Damn that cigar smoke. It was thicker inside the car than the smog he could see rising with the sunrise over the stirring city. He glanced at his partner. "Last day of the month, Harry. We can't put it off any longer. We better go shoot."

"Shoot shit," said Harry Taylor. "What a pain in the ass that rule is." He blew another cloud of dense white smoke.

"For chrissakes Harry, open the window a little. It's so smoky in here I can hardly see to drive. Besides if you don't let some air in here we'll both suffocate, or worse yet—for you anyway, there won't be enough oxygen left to keep that rope burning."

Taylor laughed and cracked the window. "O.K., that last piece of wisdom got through to me. You got to be patient with me, Jeff. At my age a lot of the old vices burn out." He waved his cigar in front of him. "Now this is one fire I can still keep lit, even though it's at the end of my cigar."

Officer Mitchell picked up the radio mike. "Squad thirty-three, request permission to qualify at the range."

"Squad thirty-three, stand by."

Harry Taylor stared at the radio receiver under the dash. "Sounds like we woke up old Steve Nelson. That was a damn grumpy reply."

"He's always grumpy, Harry. You know that. This morning at roll call he told me you taught him everything he ever knew."

"Smart ass."

Jeff laughed, picked up the mike and rogered their approval to proceed to the department range. The car slowly picked up speed as the two policemen drove west through open country towards the rolling hills on the outskirts of the city.

"Tell me, Harry, how come you don't like to shoot anymore. I've been told you used to be a helluva shot. What happened anyway?"

Another cloud of smoke enveloped the interior of the car. "More like what didn't happen I'd say." Finally he flipped the saliva drenched butt out the window. "Sure, I used to be damn good. Even was on the department pistol team. The one that used to travel around and put on exhibitions. We fired in all the Regionals and a couple of the Nationals. That was really what you call PR. You seen those trophies in the glass cases in the entryway of the station?"

Mitchell nodded as he pulled into the firing range parking lot.

"Well over half of them's mine. But that was a long time ago. The department was really great then, and police work was respected—a good job. It isn't worth a shit today."

They got out of the car and walked toward the range office. Several officers were already on the firing line and the staccato pop of the shots echoed through the hills surrounding the arroyo.

Taylor continued. "I don't know what happened. I guess I just got tired of it. They disbanded the pistol team for one thing. No incentive anymore. And hell, I been on the job now for over 30 years. I never yet drew my gun even once. Except on the range. I guess you could say I just lost interest in it."

They stepped into the range office.

"Hi, Charlie."

"Hello, Harry, Jeff. Cutting it close, aren't you waiting for the last day of the month to qualify?" The Rangemaster pushed the clipboard across the counter. "You know where to sign."

Both men signed. Name, serial number, division of assignment.

"Next line coming right up. You can go out now. Here's your ammo. Jeff, you got position number 7, Harry, you got number 8; or was that just a waste of my breath?"

Jeff Mitchell started through the door carrying a box of reloads "Coming, Harry?"

"Naaah. You go ahead. No reason to change the old M.O. at this late date. I'll stay here and keep Charlie company."

"Come on, Harry. You'll get docked a day if they catch you not shooting."

"Don't worry, partner. Old classmate Charlie will stamp me out a receipt. Won't you, Charlie?"

The Rangemaster shrugged.

"C'mon, Charlie, You owe me one, remember?"

"Oh crap, Harry, I've owed and paid that back to you out here for more years than I can count. Oh, what the hell." He time-stamped a prepunched beige card, tore off one end and handed the stub to Taylor. "Here's your receipt for monthly qualification. I just hope I never get caught doing this for you. It'll be back on the street for me."

Jeff Mitchell closed the door and smiled as he walked to his position on the line. Old time cops, he thought. All the same. A real bunch of characters all right. I'll bet old Harry Taylor hasn't fired that gun for over five years. I wonder if I'll be that way someday.

An hour and a half later they were eating breakfast at the Wagon Wheel Cafe. At 1005 hours they left the diner and walked out in the parking lot to their 19 month old squad car.

"Damn bucket of bolts," said Taylor. He opened the door, sat in the passenger seat and pulled the door closed. The door handle fell off and clattered on the carpetless floor. He picked it up and shook it at nobody in particular. "See what I mean?" he roared. "What a pile of junk. I hope we don't get a hot call. If we do, as senior officer I order you to not exceed 35 miles per hour. Promise me you will not go fast for any reason. This pile of junk would probably fall apart at forty and explode at fifty."

Jeff laughed at his partner's fury. "Hell, Harry, if you had to take the beating this thing gets 24 hours a day you would be falling apart too. And tell me. If it falls apart at forty, what's left to explode at fifty?"

"Shit, Mitchell, you sound like a sergeant. Always so technical about things. Have you ever thought why we don't get new cars? Or better cars?"

"Uh uh."

Taylor lit another cigar. The younger officer gagged and choked purposely.

"O.K., O.K., I know what the Surgeon General says. But he's too late to save me." He rolled down his window. "I'll tell you about these cars we got to drive." Taylor continued blowing great clouds of smoke as he talked. "You ever hear of those tests they do out in L.A.? Well I'll tell you. I read about them and last summer while I was fishing up at Crested Butte Lake I met a cop who gets to drive some of the cars they put through those tests. Everything I'd read was true. They really wring the cars out. Not only speed, but acceleration, steering, brakes, suspension system, the whole shmear. When they're through they have separated the real police package models from those that are just painted black and white to fool the taxpayers. Most cars don't pass the tests at all. Some of the big name makes don't even show up to be tested."

"Why not?" interrupted Mitchell.

"Cause they can't pass those tests, that's why. You know what? We're in one of those no-show failures right now. One that never passed those tests. Black and white, red lights and siren. Looks just like a real police car, don't it? It's just a piece of shit. O.K. for a family trip to the beach on a weekend, but for police work? No way. We're riding in an unsafe piece of equipment, my friend. That's the real reason they call a cop's job a hazardous occupation, because of the junk the council gives us to work with. Speaking of the council, strange isn't it, that our council president is a regular golfing buddy of the owner of a certain local automobile agency. Can you guess where our city purchasing agent bought this crap we're riding in?"

"Gee, Harry, you're really wound up today. Relax. All you're doing is feeding your ulcer again. We can't do anything about it anyway."

"Yeah I know. It's no sense bitching. I ought to know that by now. I wonder if all that has anything to do with the way I've come to feel about this job. I just don't give a damn anymore. If it wasn't for my old buddies in the department and guys like you, I'd tell them all to taking a flying . . ."

"Come on, Harry. Cool off. You're running hotter than this car. You're all burned up."

"Burned out would be more like it."

The two officers rode in silence for almost ten minutes. Then Jeff Mitchell turned and spoke. "Hey, why don't we head out a little and check Sawyer's warehouse? Remember we told them we'd try to keep an eye on the place while they closed down for their yearly all-hands two week vacation period."

"O.K." said Taylor. "Good thought. At least it'll be a line for the log."

Mitchell made a left turn at the next intersection and headed east on Industrial Avenue. At 1052 hours the two policemen arrived at the block long warehouse entrance at the corner of Industrial and Commerce Drive. Almost immediately they saw the big semi that had been backed up to the loading dock. All doors were open—on the truck and into the warehouse.

"What the hell you make of that, Jeff?"

"Don't know. But it's sure worth a check. I can't remember. Did they say they would continue deliveries during their vacation? That is one of the regular delivery trucks, isn't it?"

"Sure is, but I don't think any part of this place is supposed to be open."

Taylor gently placed the last inch and a half of his cigar on the dash ash tray. "Stay right there, you little beauty, I'll be right back." He looked at his partner. "I know the office people and the assemblers are on vacation. I thought the stockmen would be too. I guess we better check it out."

Mitchell picked up the mike. "Squad thirty-three out for investigation, 1313 Industrial Avenue." He reseated the mike and switched off the ignition. The engine bucked four times from post ignition heat then stopped. Taylor rolled his eyes skyward and muttered under his breath. Mitchell didn't bother to ask for his partner's thoughts. They got out of the car and walked towards the truck.

"I don't see a damn soul around."

Jeff nodded. "Yeah, but those doors are wide open. Somebody's got to be here."

"Coffee break maybe?"

"Maybe. Maybe not."

Jeff Mitchell touched the hood of the tractor as they walked by. "Warm, hasn't been here too long."

Taylor nodded. They walked up the concrete stairs to the large doorway and stopped. They both looked inside. Only shafts of reflected sunlight pierced the shadows in the interior of the huge building.

"Hey in there. Anybody here?" Taylor called out through cupped hands.

"I heard something. Hear it? There it is again."

Taylor shook his head. "No. What did it sound like?"

"Footsteps. Running. Then they stopped. We got to go in and take a look."

Mitchell drew his gun and stepped inside. Taylor looked at his partner, then at the gun. He shrugged his shoulders and drew his own revolver. Without thinking he blew on the gun. A small amount of dust and lint settled to the floor.

Jeff leaned over and whispered in Taylor's ear. "Let's split, but keep in sight. I'm going to call out and tell whoever is here we want to see them. But let's take a little cover first."

Taylor nodded. "Which way do you want to go?" he whispered back.

108

Jeff pointed with his gun. "You take that side of the wall, I'll take the other. Whatever we do, let's keep in sight. Let's go."

Both men moved to opposite sides of the wide passageway. "We're police officers." Jeff's voice echoed back to them from the depths of the warehouse. "Come out so we can see who you are. All we want to do is see if everything is O.K. Come out slow so nobody gets hurt."

They waited for over a minute. Harry Taylor looked at his partner. Damn, he thought, something must be wrong. If whoever was in here was legit they would've come out by now. He saw Jeff moving forward slowly and motioning him to move up even with him. After an advance of approximately twenty yards, the two officers had reached the company office spaces.

It all happened very fast.

There were many police reports documenting the events that occurred in the Sawyer warehouse on that Friday morning, the last day of February.

One of the reports was written by Officer Jeff Mitchell. Another, a highly confidential report marked *OFFICE OF THE CHIEF— ONLY,* was written by the senior homicide investigator in charge. Both reports tell the story in great detail. Pertinent parts of those reports are reproduced here:

From the report of Officer Jeffrey A. Mitchell, #2226, South Bay Division.

We were moving slowly down the passageway trying to locate

any subjects who might have been in the building. When we got to the second office space I entered and checked inside. There was no one in the office and I saw no evidence of ransacking. As I started to exit I looked through the hall window and across the passageway to where Officer Taylor was standing. He was in the doorway of another office, directly across from the one I was in. He was watching me and had his back to the inside of the office.

It was then I first saw the subject I now know as Robert (NMI) Stone. The subject was rising from behind a large desk and I could see the gun in his right hand. It was pointed at Officer Taylor. I aimed my gun at the subject but could not shoot because Officer Taylor was now directly in my line of fire. I yelled at him. I said, 'Behind you Harry, a guy with a gun.' Officer Taylor turned immediately, raised his gun and pointed it at subject Stone. I saw Officer Taylor pull the trigger. I'm sure he pulled the trigger two times. But the gun did not fire. Then the subject Stone fired two shots and Officer Taylor fell backwards into the hallway. I immediately fired all six rounds from my gun. The subject fell backwards into some cabinets. I ran over to Officer Taylor but I could see he was dead. He had been hit in the center of his forehead and once in the chest. I could tell by the wound in the head that he was dead. I checked the subject Stone. He was dead too. Then I called for help. Other officers arrived and arrested the second subject after the dogs found him hiding in the loft.

From the confidential report of Lieutenant Vincent A. La-Grand, #572, Homicide Division.

After the second suspect was arrested and the area had been processed I returned to Headquarters with the evidence that had been recovered at the scene.

During the interview with Officer Mitchell it was noted that he was of the opinion that Officer Taylor appeared to have made an attempt to fire his gun at least twice before he was shot and killed. Officer Taylor's gun was removed from the evidence locker and examined by myself and Officer Rudy Maestas of the Crime Lab. We noted the following:

The gun was a six inch .38 caliber revolver, standard for use by officers of this department. It was loaded with six live rounds of standard 158 grain round nose ammunition. The gun was extremely dirty. It was very obvious it had not been fired for a long period of time.

The barrel was very dirty and clogged with lint and dust. Several flakes of rust were removed in a subsequent cleaning by Officer Maestas.

Dust, dirt and grime filled all spaces between the side plate and frame. Two of the side plate screws had to be chiseled out with a special tool.

It was very difficult to work the crane in order to open the cylinder. The extractor star was frozen to the cylinder and the extractor rod was freed only after considerable soaking in a gun solvent.

Of the six live rounds found in the gun, two were misfires. The firing pin had made a positive strike with the cartridge primer in both instances. The misfire was caused by either a faulty firing pin or old ammunition. Tests will be conducted and a supplemental report will follow. The ammunition had to be soaked and pried out in order to unload the gun.

Officer Maestas' preliminary report indicates that in his opinion Officer Taylor did pull the trigger of his gun twice. The gun did not fire for one or more of the following reasons:

1). Old and/or deteriorated ammunition,

2). The poor condition of the weapon caused primarily by the intrusion of grime (a mixture of dirt and sweat) into those parts that must be able to move to permit proper operation of the gun.

A follow-up interview with Officer Charles Burton, Department Rangemaster, and classmate of Officer Taylor, revealed that to Burton's knowledge, Officer Taylor had not fired his weapon for monthly qualification for as long as Officer Burton has been assigned at the range. Officer Burton was transferred to the range over seven years ago, and he admitted giving Officer Taylor monthly shooting receipts. . . .

to search or not to search – there should be no question

7

to search or not to search – there should be no question

7

"Turn it up a little higher," Don Carlson told his partner. "It's really cold out tonight."

Officer Ted Blackman moved the temperature control to the right and zipped up his jacket. "Too cold for September. I hope this isn't the beginning of the kind of winter we had four years ago. I felt like I was driving around in an ice box for two months."

The police patrol car cruised east on a four-lane arterial in relatively light traffic. It had been slow the first hour, but with the bars closing, business would begin to pick up. Carlson, the driver, stopped for a red light. The light for North-South traffic flicked yellow, then red. The officers watched a metallic gold sedan enter the intersection a split second later.

"One for me," said Carlson, turning North behind the sedan. "Pretty close, but a little late. Let's have a look."

Carlson, pulled behind the violator's vehicle, flicked up the red light switch and tapped the horn ring three times.

"Looks like two in the front, two in the back. I'll take the driver, you cover."

"Okay," nodded Blackman. "I sure hate to get out though. Damn, it's cold tonight."

"Hi," said Carlson. He stood slightly behind the young male driver and flashed his light on the three young passengers. He quickly glanced up and could see Blackman standing to the right and slightly to the rear of their car. All kids, he thought, two boys with their dates out for the evening. The driver looked up at Carlson and said nothing.

"May I see your license, please?"

"The light was yellow when I went through it," the young driver blurted out. The three heads in the car nodded silently in definite agreement.

Carlson smiled. He glanced at the two young faces in the rear seat. It was hard to tell which one had the most lipstick smeared on which face. There was no way those two would have known what color the lights had been at any intersection their friend had driven through. Oh well, he thought, help your buddy, nothing wrong with that. He had done the same more than once.

"Just show me your driver's license and the registration for the car, then we'll talk about it."

118

The young man quickly offered the registration slip and his license to the officer. "It was yellow. We all saw it. Is it against the law to go through on the yellow?"

Carlson looked at the information on the license and began writing on a white card. "No it's not. Now, let me tell you what I am going to do." He bent forward and addressed the young people in the car. "You all say Mr. Burns went through on the yellow. My partner and I think you just missed the yellow and went through on the red. What I want to do is what the man says on TV—let's make a deal, okay?"

"What kind of a deal?" asked the driver. "I don't get it."

"An easy one. I want you to know that I do sincerely believe you went through the red light. I admit it was close. The deal is, I don't write you a citation and you be careful and try not to come that close again—how about it?"

"Yeah, that's a deal." The young man smiled. Then he was concerned once more, "What're you writing?"

"Okay," said the officer. "A fair question deserves a fair answer. I'll show you what I wrote so you will understand." He handed the driver the 3x5 white card. "That's called a Field Contact Card, Mr. Burns. It's a record that I did talk to you but it's not the kind of police record people don't like. Nothing like that. It's necessary that policemen keep track of what they do, who we talk to, and where we are. The card will be filed in a special drawer for about a year and then it will be destroyed. But it is not a police arrest record. Now you give that card back and I'll give you one to keep. This is my personal business card, my name, the district I work, and the phone number. Now you all be careful and have a good time, okay?"

"Yeah, okay, no more close ones—even on the yellow."

Carlson laughed and walked back to the police car. Blackman was already inside and shivering.

"Damn it's cold. Why did you take so long with those kids anyway if you weren't going to write them?" He began entering the Field Contact Card information in their log.

Carlson started the car and pulled out into the light traffic. "Lots of reasons. First, it makes the job easier to get along with people, right?"

"Agreed," said Blackman. "But you can't stop writing tickets."

"Don't intend to," replied Carlson. "But each case is different. That was a close one. We know that kid went through on the red, and maybe he knows it too. But maybe he really believes it was yellow. Anyway it was close. I've a gut feeling he'll react the way I hope he does and will be a better driver because of it, and I think we made a couple of friends."

Blackman looked up. "I guess that's the police discretion thing the lieutenant was talking about last night at roll call. Right?"

"Right," said Carlson. "The law is not all black and white. Unfortunately, some policemen think so and they're wrong. You know them and I know them. Guys right in our own division. Discretion can be used as long as it's done using good judgment and common sense." Carlson paused and they listened as the dispatcher announced a purse snatch in progress. The call was given to a unit on the south end of town, well out of their patrol area.

Carlson continued. "The lieutenant defined it pretty well I

thought when he said, 'the use of discretion depends on the dynamics of the situation.'"

"That's what he said alright," nodded Blackman. "Exactly. You sure got a good memory. You'll probably be a lieutenant yourself someday."

"More than that I hope," smiled Carlson. "Have you ever heard the Chief do the one on police discretion and why policemen don't cite other policemen?"

Blackman shook his head. "No. He could convince me, but how can he convince a bunch of citizens it's okay not to write other cops?"

"You should hear him." Carlson turned west, then turned into a driveway and cruised slowly, lights out, by the closed doors of a huge shopping complex. "I went to one of his monthly citizen meetings one night about two months ago. A guy in the audience stood up, waved a ticket at the Chief, and asked him if he had been a cop, would he have received the ticket. He admits going 47 in a 35 but he's heard cops don't write the other cops tickets. How come?—he says?"

"Wow" replied Blackman. "I wouldn't know how to answer that one."

Carlson laughed. "That's why he's the Chief and you're here with me."

Both men waved to a night cleanup crew foreman. Carlson pulled on the headlight switch and the patrol car reentered the main stream of traffic.

"Well, first the Chief sets them up. He asks how many really believe everyone who commits a traffic violation should get a ticket. Naturally almost all of them raise their hands."

Blackman grinned, "Did you?" he asked.

"Hell no, I'd seen him do this before. Anyway, now he's got everybody on record that if you blow a stop sign, you got a ticket coming. Then he asks, does anyone think it's possible to drive a car without eventually committing a traffic violation, even a small one, he says, like running a stop sign? Well, everybody knows they have so they all agree that everybody has at one time or another committed a traffic violation. Then the Chief sets up what he calls a hypothetical situation. He tells the audience to make believe they're all police officers. Now he tells them, you're out on patrol and you've stopped at a stop sign controlled intersection. It's about 1 AM, very light traffic. You see a car drive through, not high speed, but no slowing down either. Right through the red stop sign. Now you've stopped the car. The driver's a policeman from upstate. You don't know him, but he's a police officer. Then the Chief asks how many think they would write him a ticket?"

"All the hands go up," interrupts Blackman.

"Right," responds Carlson. "Okay, says the Chief, now it's the next night and you're on patrol. Same thing happens, same time, same place, but different violator's car. Right through the stop sign. This time you know the driver, it's your regular partner who is off on a week's vacation. How many of you would write your partner? He's the man you work with almost every night, check out burglars, robbers, walk dark alleys with and eat with while you're working. Lots of hands still go up, but maybe not so many this time. Then the Chief does it again, same thing but this time the driver is your neighbor, your best friend. You play golf twice a month with him. He and his whole family are coming

122

over to your house for a Bar-B-Q next weekend, but he's gone through the stop sign. How many of you will cite your best friend and neighbor, he asks. Still lots of hands but not so many."

"Yeah, I can see it coming," said Blackman. "The next one stopped is probably the Chief himself."

"No, I think the old man is too smart for that. The next one is your wife. Then the next one is your mother-in-law. Now he's got a lot less hands and he has them laughing. Most are starting to see the light but he's still got a few die-hards. The Chief goes through it again and the next driver who goes through the stop sign is your own mother. He's just about got them whipped. The guy that started this is still in the game but when he holds up his hand that he would cite his own mother, he catches a lot of dirty looks from the audience.

"Then the Chief wipes him out. He says, okay, now sir, you've had a pretty rough week. You've cited an upstate policeman, your partner, your best friend, your wife, your mother-in-law and even your own mother. You're a great humanist, old "law-and-order" they call you back at the station house. Now you're on your way home after a hard week's work for a nice two days off. You're tired, it will be good to get home and relax. Suddenly as you're driving, you look about you, then you get sort of a queasy feeling in your stomach. You just realized that in your preoccupied state of mind, you yourself have driven right through the stop sign at the same intersection where you wrote all those nice folks this past week. Now, sir, says the Chief, do you stop and issue yourself a citation? I remember you agreeing that everyone who commits a traffic violation should receive a citation but now there is only one police officer around who saw the violation and that's you."

"Jeez, I'd like to have been there," nodded Blackman.

It was beautiful to watch," said Carlson. "The Chief ended up by telling the people everybody is human and cops are certainly not a bunch of robots. He makes sure to tell them two things, though. To cite or not is up to us. If we feel another cop's got it coming, it's up to us. We have that discretion. He also reminds them that police officers who do commit serious violations, drunk driving, reckless, and stuff like that, most often have a rougher time of it than any other citizen, particularly if it's one of his officers."

"Amen," responded Blackman.

Carlson slowed and pulled into the "24-Hour Pantry" parking lot. "How about dinner?" he asked his partner.

"Okay,"Blackman said. "What a crazy life. You order dinner if you want. I'm ordering breakfast. I just hope it's warm in there."

Forty-five minutes later, the two officers were back on patrol. At 0215 hours they stopped a big Imperial and Carlson cited the driver, 20 over in a 35. At 0225 hours, Carlson pointed ahead and said, "There's one for you, partner, you're next up to write one."

Blackman nodded. He too had seen the panel truck exit the back alley and turn North about a half-block ahead of them.

"I'll take it. Man, it's really dark out. That guy should know he's driving without lights."

"Yeah," replied Carlson. "And I'd like to know what he was doing in that alley. You write the ticket and I'll check him for warrants, and that plate for stolen."

124

Carlson reached over and flipped the switch. The glare of the red lights flashed on the truck as it slowed and stopped at the curb. The two policemen got out of their car. As they started forward, the driver stepped out and walked towards them. He was young, early 20's, medium size, slacks, dark windbreaker.

"What's the problem? Sure couldn't be speed."

"Nope" said Carlson. "But even at safe speeds, you've got to have lights on at 2:30 in the morning."

"Damn, I must have really been daydreaming."

"Night dreaming, I'd call it," said Blackman. "Let's see your driver's license and registration."

The young man felt his pockets. "Shit. I had a feeling it was going to be a lousy night. I forgot my license.

Must be home or at my girl friend's house." He moved his hands over his waist and outside his pockets again. "I don't have a damn thing on me," he said.

"That's count two," said Carlson. "By the way, what were you doing in the alley?"

"Just a shortcut, man. Just cutting through to get out of the traffic. That's O.K. isn't it?"

"If that's all you were doing." Carlson looked at his partner. "What do you want to do?"

Blackman shivered and pulled his collar up higher on his neck. "It looks like we got a bit of checking to do. Let's get out of the cold and finish this up in the car. I'll write him up while you check him out." Then motioning to the young man, Blackman said, "O.K., let's get in the car and have a talk." The man shrugged his shoulders and followed the officer. Blackman opened the rear door of the police cruiser and the man got in, sliding over to the center of the rear seat. The officers entered and sat on the front seat.

Blackman turned, pencil poised over his citation book. "Last name?"

"Ward."

"First name?"

"John," said the man in the back seat slouching forward.

"Got a middle name?"

"Franklin."

"Date of birth?"

"Uhhh . . . June first."

"How about a year?"

"1948."

"How tall are you?" Blackman noted his partner was writing down the man's answers on an F.C. card.

"About five foot ten," came the almost whispered reply.

"Your weight?"

"One fifty five."

"Address?"

The man in the back seat mumbled a reply. Both officers stopped writing and looked up. How the hell can a guy sweat so much on a cold night like this?, thought Blackman. Carlson reached forward and lifted the microphone up and out of its clip. "Speak up, tell the man your address."

"I'm staying at a motel."

"What motel?" asked Blackman. "Motels have addresses."

"It's on South Broadway."

"South Broadway is a long street. What's the number of the place?"

The young man responded and watched as Carlson spoke into the microphone. "Car twenty-three requests check for want and record."

The dispatcher acknowledged and Carlson continued. "Want and record on Ward, John Franklin. Male Caucasian. D.O.B. six one forty-eight, five ten, one fifty-five, brown and brown." Then peering at the license plate on the panel truck in front of him, "Also registration and stolen on X-ray William six zero four two zero . . ."

The voice from the back seat was so low the officers barely heard him. "That did it, pigfuckers."

The policemen looked up at the man who sat alone behind them.

He was holding a two inch 38 caliber revolver and shifting the muzzle slowly back and forth from the head of Carlson to the head of Blackman.

"Keep your hands in sight. Do what I say. No fast moves. No way am I going back to the joint." Pointing the gun at Carlson he said, "Start driving, mother. Just normal. No high speed. No sudden stops. Keep your hands on the wheel. Both of them." Then pointing the gun at Blackman, "You, look straight ahead. Put both hands on your knees. Palms down. Keep them there."

Carlson, mentally cursing himself for substituting comfort for safety, pulled slowly out from the curb and drove North.

"Take a right at the corner. Easy."

Carlson stopped at the corner and glanced to the right, then to the left.

"Keep looking straight ahead, cop, no looking or talking to your friend."

"Christ man, I got to look down a street before I turn." Carlson turned slowly and headed east.

"Just shut up and drive. Turn right at the next corner, take another right down that alley." Carlson turned the police cruiser south then west into the alley.

"Now stop the car," said the man with the gun. "Right here." The patrol car stopped. Jesus, Carlson thought, this is the alley we saw him come out of. He's going to get out, go back to his parked truck and cut out. But he knows we'll be right on him, unless he is going to . . . Carlson's sudden realization of his planned execution was verified by the familiar click of a revolver hammer being cocked just behind his head.

"Jump, Ted," shouted Carlson, as he pushed in the headlight switch, opened the door and rolled out of the car into the darkness. Carlson heard successive shots, heard his partner scream, and saw the flashes from the gun light up the alley as he rolled under the car and drew his revolver.

It was quiet for a few seconds. Then Carlson heard the left rear door open and saw the legs of the man who had been in the back seat emerge. The gunman began to walk rapidly away from the car. Quickly the officer crawled out from the car, stood up, reached inside the car and turned on the headlights.

"Stop where you are or I'll shoot." Carson saw the man turn and raise his gun. Both fired at the same time, the suspect wildly at the blinding headlights and Carlson deliberately at the well-lighted figure. The man staggered and fell backwards after the officer pulled the trigger the second time.

For all practical purposes, the story of Officers Carlson and Blackman is complete. I have told this story many times to various groups of police officers: rookies, inservice training veterans, and supervisors. Even the rookies know where the error was made. But policemen are curious and I have learned long ago that their curiosity must be satisfied or the thoughts of "what happened afterwards" will detract from the desired learning process: that a subject under any kind of suspicion must be thoroughly searched; particularly before being placed in a police car for interview, interrogation or transportation.

In the story just related, suspect Ward, a wanted parole violator, died four hours later in the emergency room of the County Hospital. Officer Carlson was uninjured. Officer Blackman, moving much more slowly than his partner, was shot in the back and is partially paralyzed for life.

Police officer apathy relating to proper search is not only a perplexing problem, it can be deadly and tragic. It has been my experience that most department policies usually ignore searching procedures. As a result the policeman in the field will or will not search depending on his own judgment and initiative. The preponderance of evidence in police shooting tragedies should certainly satisfy the rational man theory that police officers have the right to conduct a thorough search any time the situation permits a lawful search.

I believe the police officer should search for weapons whenever:

1. A police officer suspects a subject is armed;
2. A subject under arrest is placed in a police vehicle, for transportation, interrogation or interview;
3. An unknown subject is being detained and must, for some good and *proper* reason, be placed in a police vehicle during the interview.

A poor search, or no search at all, coupled with poor handcuff procedures (a subject to be discussed later) accounts for a tragically high number of officers killed each year.

It is true that there are a greater number of officers killed answering felony in progress calls and while making traffic stops. The difference is that in felony in progress and traffic stop situations, some deaths are unavoidable. In those cases where the officers died because of a poor search or poor handcuff technique, none of the deaths were unavoidable. All deaths in these instances could have been prevented by:

1. Sound department policy regarding search and use of hand-

130

cuffs;
2. Training in proper search and handcuff procedures;
3. Strict supervision and enforcement of the policy and procedures established;
4. Adherence to policy and procedures regarding proper search
   and use of handcuffs by all personnel.

There are many cases, too many unfortunately, of police officer
deaths due to poor search or no search at all. The following cases
are selected because the errors are dissimilar. But the end result,
death for the officer, was the same in each case of improper
search.

Obviously all persons contacted do not have to be searched. Nice
people get into difficulty with the law in "very routine" situations. But sometimes people who are not so nice get into difficulty with the law in situations that may appear to be "very
routine."

For example:

The state trooper on a rural beat received a radio call to investigate a traffic accident. On arriving at the scene, he saw a single
vehicle run-off-the-highway type of accident.

A rural route mailman had discovered the demolished car
against a large cottonwood and had called from a nearby farm-
house. The three men—the mailman, the farmer, and the
trooper—helped the dazed middle-aged driver out of the wreck.
The man did not appear to be seriously injured. He told his
rescuers he must have fallen asleep after having driven for a long
time, almost 24 hours without a stop for a rest. His destination,
he said, was a city on the coast. He asked for a ride and the
trooper agreed to take the man as far as headquarters where
further transportation could be arranged. The trooper made

notes of the accident scene and assisted the still somewhat dazed driver into his car and left.

What actually happened during the ride will forever be unknown. The trooper's car was first discovered abandoned, then the body of the trooper was found. He had been shot to death. His gun was still in his holster and had not been fired.

The subject was later apprehended and committed to a state institution for the insane. The car he had been driving was stolen and had been used by the subject to commit several armed robberies after his escape from a hospital in a neighboring state.

This incident should establish a simple fact police officers sometimes too easily forget. Criminals, hard core criminals, and mentally deranged persons, can also get involved in traffic accidents, inadvertently drive through red lights, and commit other seemingly inoffensive acts classified as "minor violations."

In another case of poor search, but a different type of error, the results were still the same: a police officer funeral.

The officer was assigned duty in a one-man car. While driving by a small market he saw a young man run from a store with the manager in pursuit. The officer had no problem in apprehending the fleeing subject. He walked his prisoner back to the manager who advised the officer that the young man had tried to take a carton of cigarettes without paying for them. The alleged thief turned to the officer and said he had just picked up the cigarettes when the manager had yelled at him and he had dropped the carton on the floor. When asked by the policeman why he had run, the youngster said the manager had scared him.

The manager then advised the officer that he had seen the subject in the store several times just looking around, and that he

132

never bought anything. He was sure he was casing the place or getting ready to steal something. The policeman said he'd take the subject to the station for questioning and to be checked out.

The youngster pleaded with the officer, saying the last time he'd been in any kind of trouble like this, the policeman had merely given him a ticket and he went to court later and paid a fine. Why couldn't he just get a ticket instead of going to jail?

The officer's last words were, "We don't give tickets for shoplifting in this city, let's go . . ." The petty thief then turned instant felon. He drew a gun from under his shirt and fatally shot the officer.

Again we have a situation that did not appear to be "serious." In the above case, the officer never searched the subject. Perhaps he thought a petty thief would not be armed or that a youngster is not dangerous.

Do juveniles shoot policemen? Yes, very definitely they do. In 1972 eight persons under 18 years of age murdered policemen. The youngest was 13. In 1973 it wasn't all that bad. Only seven officers were murdered by juveniles and the youngest was 15. In 1974, ten officers were murdered by persons under 18, the two youngest involved were 15 and 14 years old. Without relating the details of these cases, I think the statistics give clear and convincing proof that police officers should be permitted to search and handcuff the juveniles they must take into custody.

In another case:

At roll call a two-man radio car team received information that a local subject known to them was wanted for a CCW charge. A warrant had been issued and an attached report indicated the subject was still known to be carrying the concealed weapon.

Later that same day, the officers observed the subject standing on a street corner next to a pawn shop. The surviving officer recalls the conversation.

His partner, he said, remarked that the wanted man had probably just sold the gun to the pawn shop dealer. He acknowledged the warrant still required an arrest. As the policemen approached the man, he attempted to flee, but was easily apprehended. A search was conducted and the officers were surprised when they found the gun under his shirt behind the belt buckle. As they stopped their search momentarily to unload the little derringer the subject pulled a second gun, one that he had just bought in the pawn shop, and the close range eight shot fire fight began. One officer died and the other was wounded. The suspect was killed by the surviving officer.

All police officers will say they are aware of the lesson in this case; it's obvious. A proper search must be made. But a proper search is a complete search. Finding one weapon does not mean there isn't a second, or even a third hidden within the subject's reach. All police officers know that.

Then why did I have to go to that funeral?

There isn't a working police officer around who wouldn't agree that the family dispute call is fraught with danger. Unquestionably this type of call is also very frustrating.

In the following tragic case, two police officers on duty in a two-man car received a call, "See the woman, a family dispute, and a man with a gun."

It might be well to stop and reflect for a moment on the "man with a gun" information. Certainly a good dispatcher should advise the field officer if it's known that a gun or other weapon has been used or seen. But is it really necessary to be reminded that a gun might be close by in any circumstance or situation? Without even knowing the number of guns in the United States, police officers everywhere should realize there is an excellent chance one or more guns could be in any home, place of business, or car, on every call to which they must respond. Count on it. Be alert for it.

Back to the story.

The officers drove to the address, parked their car and walked up two flights of stairs in the three story apartment hotel. After just two knocks on the door it was opened and the lady of the house invited them in. There was no question that a family dispute had occurred. The woman's eyes were red and swollen, her nose obviously broken and bleeding, and her dress was in shreds. She pointed to the man sitting on the couch. He was wearing slacks, T shirt, socks, no shoes. "Take him away," she said. "Far away and never bring him back. He has beaten me for the last time. I never want to see him again."

The officers looked at each other knowingly and shrugged their shoulders. The man looked at his wife, sipped from a can of beer, looked at the officers and said, "Fine with me, but I'm staying. Let her leave."

While one officer completed the assault report the other questioned the husband. "No," he said, "I got no record. Nothing that counts for anything. Went to jail once for drunk but that was almost twenty years ago. I'm a hard working man. Work 50 to 60 hours a week at the local lumber mill. She's just pissed because I want to watch the ball game. When she started to dump my beer down the drain I whacked her a couple of times. She'll get over it. Always has before."

The reporting officer completed his report and asked the wife to sign. The second officer turned to the man and advised him his wife had signed the complaint. The policeman then pointed towards the bedroom and said, "Go get your shoes and a shirt on. You're going to jail."

The man sat motionless on the couch. Then he looked at his wife and shook his head.

"Let's go man," said one officer. "It's almost end of watch. I want to get you locked up so I can go home. Get something on, it's getting cold outside."

Then without a word the husband stood and walked slowly into his bedroom alone. A few moments later he re-entered the living room. He was carrying a rifle. The rifle the wife had told the police complaint clerk her husband had used to "whack" her with. Before the startled policemen could react he shot and killed both of them.

It seems axiomatic that policemen would know that proper search techniques include a procedure whereby a subject, taken into custody, and who needs clothing—or anything—is given the items he needs only after the officer has obtained and searched the articles. But policemen do it wrong time and time again. Most are lucky and there are no weapons in the clothing. This sort of tragedy, however, occurs too frequently.

There are some policemen who are lucky. Not very smart, just very lucky. In the following case, "Officer Lucky" had stopped a drunk driver.

Just prior to being transported to jail, the arrestee asked if he might get his cigarettes out of his car. "Certainly," replied the agreeable and naive "Officer Lucky." Thirty seconds later, the

136

officer was in a fire fight for his life with the DUI, who had picked up an automatic concealed under the front seat of the car. The suspect was killed in this case by "Officer Lucky," who miraculously escaped being shot. So the officer was lucky. But what else was he?

Then there is the "Unlucky Officer." In this instance the officer was assigned a traffic warrants detail. Some people just won't pay up, so warrants must be issued. The officer went to the scofflaw's house. The subject was home and was advised he must go to jail. "What's the bail?" asked the arrestee, familiar with the procedure.

"A hundred and five dollars," replied the officer.

"Let me get it, okay? I'll be right out."

The policeman agreed and waited. Again, the vicious fire fight. This time there were no fatalities. The suspect would recover from his wounds and spend the next six years of his life in prison. The twenty-four year old officer would also recover from his wounds. But he would also spend the rest of his life in bed, paralyzed from his waist to his toes.

The last case I wish to discuss is the classic tragedy relating to search.

Officer Bob Whitehead was close to being the ideal patrolman. Bob Whitehead was a World War II veteran, a combat veteran who had twice parachuted behind enemy lines and fought his way back to friendly lines, wrecking enemy installations along the way. He'd been a policeman for over five years and loved his job.

Whitehead was a supervisor's delight: he was never a problem, walked a beat, rode a radio car; whatever the assignment, he did it and he did it well. No complaints.

Bob was also used as a field training officer and most all the young officers in the district who had come under his watchful eye were better men because of him.

Citizen contact and his production in the field could not be faulted. His citations, FI Cards, felony and misdemeanor arrests were either tops or near the top, month after month. Wherever he patrolled, he was respected. The business community liked him around, but realized and accepted the fact that Officer Bob Whitehead played no favorites. "Stay legal," was his quiet warning to the neighborhood tough, or the businessman who might have had thoughts of breaking the law to increase his financial station in life.

The incident occurred early on a Friday night. Officer Bob Whitehead had been assigned to walk a beat in an older section of the city, a neighborhood of older homes skirted by small stores and the typical neighborhood tavern.

Around 9:00 PM, the owner-bartender of one of the taverns threw down his bar towel and walked angrily out the front door looking for the officer he'd seen walk by not twenty minutes ago. "Hey, Bob," he called. The officer, across the street, turned from his conversation with the dwarfed and crippled newsstand operator, and waved to the tavern owner. "Be right there," he said.

Whitehead told his small friend he would see him later and walked across the street and into the bar.

"This guy is a real problem, Bob," said the owner pointing to a middle-aged, round shouldered man sitting at the end of the counter. "He's bad mouthing everything and everybody. Started with the weather, now it's my customers. Some of them have left and told me to let them know when this guy is gone."

"Is he drunk?" said the officer.

"Hell, no. I wouldn't be serving him if he was, you know that. He's just creepy. I need the business, but he's costing me business."

"Want to make an arrest for disorderly?"

"No, Bob. How about just explaining the rules to the guy. Maybe if you talk to him, he'll quiet down."

"Okay, let's use your office in the back. Come with me."

The policeman and owner walked up to the man on the last stool.

"Howdy," said the policeman. "I want to talk to you for a minute. Let's go in the back office." The man shrugged his shoulders, stood up and followed the manager into his office. The officer trailed behind. With the door closed, the officer directed the man to turn around and raise his hands.

"I'm clean for crissakes."

"I'm going to make sure of it," Whitehead responded. The search was thorough. Officer Whitehead had conducted thousands of searches and had recovered just about every kind of weapon that could possibly be concealed on a human body.

"Okay, you're clean. Now, what's the problem?"

"I just don't like the place, that's all. I don't like your goddamn city and I don't like him," the man nodded toward the bartender.

The officer completed an FI card and said, "Why not leave then. Might be a good idea. If you stay and create a fuss, this man can arrest you for disorderly. Then I'll have to take you to jail. Either behave yourself or leave. Get it?"

"Show me the door, cop, and I'm gone, this place is a crummy dump anyhow."

"Show him the door, Stan, I guess he wants to leave."

"Right," said the owner. He opened his office door. The trouble-maker walked out the front door without looking back or stopping.

"Thanks Bob, appreciate it. What a creep."

"Okay, Stan, see you later."

It was less than thirty minutes later when Bob Whitehead, a block away discussing a shoplifting problem with a market manager, was told by a local resident that Stan wanted him back. The message was, "Tell Bob that creep is in my place again."

The officer sighed and started back. As he approached the tavern he could see Stan out front waiting for him.

Stan was angry and upset. "That creepy little bastard has come back. I tried to be nice to him. Gave him a beer on the house. Wouldn't you know, he dumped most of it on the floor. Said he didn't drink warm beer. It's darn near ice cold. Almost everybody left. Get him out of here, Bob. I'll sign the complaint."

"Okay, I'll take him across the street to the corner call box and get a district car."

The officer entered and was greeted with a stream of profanity from the lone but unwanted patron. "Let's go," said the patrolman. "I told you to behave. Now this man is arresting you for disorderly conduct. I'm going to call a car and take you to jail. It's your own doing. Get up, we're going to take a walk across the street."

Grasping the man's right elbow, Bob Whitehead easily lead the arrestee out of the tavern, across the street and down the corner to the call box attached to the telephone pole. "Now don't run away," said the officer.

The little man, suddenly quiet, watched as the officer released the large bronze key from his Sam Browne belt, inserted it in the call box door and reached in to pick up the phone. Then, just as quietly, the man drew a large automatic from inside his waistband, pointed it at the officer and started pulling the trigger.

The officer was speaking into the phone, "Whitehead here Oscar. Send a wagon or car to meet me at Seventh Avenue and Flower. I got a . . . oh, Christ, I've been shot, he's . . ." The officer at the station heard the roar of the gun on the phone. He put it down quickly and spoke into the base station radio at his desk, "All units in the vicinity Seventh Avenue and Flower, a shooting and an officer down, code three. All units . . ."

Five minutes later an emergency hospital ambulance attendant stood at the corner and wrote "police officer" and "DOA" after the printed words "victim" and "condition" in his call record book. Then he reached down and gently pulled away the little newspaper vendor who was kneeling and sobbing uncontrollably over the uniformed figure under the sheet in the gutter. A police sergeant rode up and called out to the ambulance crew. "One of you better come with me. Bring your black bag, too. A bunch of the neighborhood citizens caught the guy that shot Bob and they've half beat him to death. It took three of us to get him away from them."

The disfigured little newsman, tears streaking down his face looked at the Sergeant and screamed loudly, "Why stop them? Why? Why?"

When this story is told to a group of officers, I follow with a question. "If this had been you, what would you have done differently?" There is, of course, a chorus of replies. All the same and all correct. "I would've searched the man again on second contact."

Certainly that is the correct answer. The subject in this instance left after the first contact, went to his nearby car and armed himself. Undoubtedly, his sick brain was now convinced that he was all powerful. Back to his tormentors to teach them a lesson. Of course, the officer should have searched him on second contact. It should be a golden rule for all police officers to research any time an arrestee or suspect is recontacted.

Then to my class of policemen I propound a sobering thought.

"I want to ask you two questions," I tell them. "Don't answer now, just think about the answers. But think about them for a long time. For as long as you are police officers."

"I told you all what kind of a man and what kind of a policeman Bob Whitehead was. A World War II combat veteran, trained to survive behind the enemy lines. A veteran patrol officer who was never known to make a mistake. A training officer for probationary police officers."

Then I ask my first question. "How many of you, seriously now, how many of you have all of those qualifications?" The class gets the point. None of them raise their hands.

My second question follows. "It did happen to him. As good as he was, Officer Bob Whitehead was allowed only one mistake. How many will you be allowed?"

In closing, I repeat, and tell the class, "You should think of your answers to those two questions for a long time. It could be worth your while to do so. Perhaps, even worth your life."

the deadly combination: no search, no handcuffs

8

the deadly combination: no search, no handcuffs

8

The causes surrounding violent death and serious injury to police officers resulting from an improper search are similar to the improper use of handcuffs. Several of these causes are:

1. Apathy, carelessness, preoccupation, overconfidence. It does not matter which term is used, but inattention during a search, or indifference to proper use of handcuffs, has resulted in at least embarrassment or injury to thousands of "lucky" police officers—and tragic and unnecessary deaths to hundreds of others.

2. Policy, procedure, rules and training. There appears to be only a few law enforcement agencies that have documented policy, procedure or rules regarding search and use of handcuffs. Only a very small percentage of all departments provide adequate training in search and handcuff procedures.

147

It is most certainly true that the deaths of many police officers killed responding to felony in progress situations may be classed as "unpreventable." However, in almost every instance (if the case is properly investigated and reconstructed, and all facts are reported) in which a police officer was murdered during a search or use of handcuff situation, the death can be classed as "preventable."

There are a surprising number of cases resulting in death or serious injury to police officers in incidents where the subject was not handcuffed after being taken into custody by a police officer. It is even more surprising when most cases show that the arrestee was in custody for robbery, burglary, auto theft, rape, ADW, or CCW. In several instances the arresting officer was attempting to transport two felony suspects when he was murdered.

Research and analysis of police officer shootings reveal a remarkably high number of incidents where police officers were killed by persons in custody for misdemeanors but who had not been properly searched or handcuffed. High on this list of police killers would be those initially arrested for drunk related offenses. Recently lawmakers in several states have mandated the public drunk as a sick person, not to be arrested, but still taken into custody. To argue the merits of this legislation, legally, medically, or sociologically, would be inappropriate at this time. There should be no question however, that the noncriminal public drunk has been diverted from a major segment of the criminal justice system—the courts. But he is still a problem for the police segment of the system.

The drunk must be taken into custody by the police either as a misdemeanant or as a sick person. It is discouraging to hear a few police officers say, "Let them lay, they want to be that way." This attitude is not only unprofessional, it is inhuman. It may also lead to an unnecessary waste of police manpower. It has

148

been my experience that the total time consumed in picking up and processing a drunk is considerably less than if the drunk is left to be robbed or murdered. Experienced homicide investigators everywhere know that "wino murders" are seldom if ever solved. And every wino found lying in an alley with his skull caved in still counts "one" in that top statistic column entitled CRIME INDEX OFFENSES.

Thus, the decriminalized drunk has not been diverted from the police segment of the criminal justice system. The drunk must be taken into custody for his own safety. Those who complain of being sick or injured must be taken to a hospital for treatment. Reports must be completed by the officer to document his contact with the subject—for many obvious and good reasons; for example, property must be placed in safekeeping.

Proposals to employ nonpolice type persons to respond to drunk calls are as naive a suggestion as having them respond to barking dog complaints. Drunks have killed armed police officers. What chance would the unarmed civilian have? As for barking dogs— why is the dog barking? The reason could demand a response by an armed police officer.

Something to think about: The search of a "decriminalized" drunk. A proper (legal) search of the drunk taken into custody, but not arrested, will eventually require a judicial decision regarding the legality of recovering contraband after searching a person who is not being "arrested." The tragedy of police officers killed statistics should leave no doubt that the drunk taken into custody, arrested or not, must be searched and searched thoroughly. Not just frisked, but searched for the officer's protection. This procedure should be policy in all police departments.

Contraband discovered during a search of a "decriminalized"

drunk is a matter of local policy to be solved by the prosecutor's office or the courts. A recommended procedure for police requires that the facts be presented to the local prosecutor for disposition—after the drunk has been searched.

I would hope that by now I have convinced the police officer reading this text that prisoners must be handcuffed and thoroughly searched. Unfortunately, many police officers do use handcuffs and are still killed or injured by prisoners.

Handcuffing the subject in front, without securing the cuffs to a strong belt or preferably to a light steel chain, is only slightly more effective than no handcuffs at all. The subject, handcuffed in front, now has in his hands a dangerous or even a deadly weapon. Many police officers who read these lines will remember, then reach up and feel the scars left by the handcuffs that were raked across their face. Or they may be able to rattle their dentures around and sadly recall that permanent teeth used to be where now these clacking ivories slip.

But there have been more serious cases. Handcuffs secured in front have been used as a garrote, a garrote supplied by the victim officer. The most frequent tragedy usually runs: the handcuffed suspect, who has been poorly searched, notes that the officer is relaxed and not very attentive. The suspect then reaches out and disarms the officer or surreptitiously removes a hidden weapon and shoots the officer.

Boots have been used many times to hide a small gun. More than just once, a gun has been removed from a boot and used to murder a police officer after an arrest and after a "search."

The transportation of prisoners can be dangerous, with the problems apparently a composite of officers being over confident and too relaxed while performing the routine and uneventful chore of prisoner transfer between jails, or between jail and hospital.

A review of three years, 1972, 1973, and 1974, in the FBI publication of "Law Enforcement Officers Killed Summary," reveals many police officer murders committed while performing routine prisoner transportation assignments. A review over many years reflects even more unnecessary and avoidable deaths. In most cases, the officers were disarmed and shot with their own weapons. It seems impossible that if the prisoners had been properly handcuffed or restrained these killings would have occurred.

Contrary to the opinion of a few persons and groups, most police officers neither seek out violence nor like to embarrass people with their lawful authority. Most police officers attempt to resolve conflict peaceably and treat others with compassion. At times this trait has resulted in a police officer's death. The instances just mentioned are examples. Undoubtedly, the good men killed transporting prisoners were not following safety procedures, and the attempt to show compassion for prisoners during the transfer proved a fatal mistake.

The concluding case is a classic tragedy.

The detective had completed his extradition proceedings and picked up his prisoner at the County Jail. Before the ride to the airport the officer explained the rules to his prisoner, "Behave yourself and we'll have an easy trip home. I don't want to embarrass you by putting these cuffs on behind your back, but I have to put them on; it's department policy. If you promise to take it easy, I'll just put them on in front. You can cover them with your coat sleeves and even smoke, O.K.?"

The prisoner agreed there would be no trouble. The detective and his prisoner were driven to the airport. There was a 45 minute wait until boarding time. A half hour after arriving at the airport the man asked the officer if he could get a drink of water. They both walked to the water fountain and the man reached out with cuffed hands, turned the handle and drank. When he finished the officer leaned over, turned the handle and took a drink. The prisoner suddenly reached out, drew the detective's gun from its holster and shot the officer twice.

There are exceptions to every rule. On occasions I have not handcuffed a felon in my custody. Once, after two hours of interrogation and admissions of involvement in two murders, several armed robberies, and many burglaries, a subject asked me for coffee. The request was granted.

I escorted the man, who'd been in jail and searched again prior to interrogation, to the crowded cafeteria on the top floor of the police building, but not in handcuffs. Many police officers have done the same thing, and it is appropriate for the occasion for obvious reasons. However, when the prisoner was transported the following day in a police car to the County Jail just three blocks away for arraignment, he was searched again and handcuffed to a waist chain.

Department policy should require all felony prisoners and felony arrestees to be handcuffed properly when they are transported. Usually in the case of misdemeanants the use of handcuffs is at the discretion of the officer; use of handcuffs should be encouraged, however, and intoxicated persons should always be handcuffed.

152

The deadly combination is neither to search nor to handcuff. Whenever suspects are transported without a search or minus handcuffs, it should be scored as "pure luck" for the officer who accomplishes this feat without suffering injury or death. The next best (or next worst?) is to do only one, search or handcuff, particularly handcuff in front. Score this procedure as "pretty lucky" if accomplished without incident.

To preclude "luck," establish department policy and procedures and provide training for police officers on proper search and handcuff methods.

I am unaware of a single case of a police officer being killed or seriously injured by a subject who had been properly searched and handcuffed.

taking a
bad position

9

taking a
bad position

It has been said that the patrol car is one of the best defensive weapons for the police officer working the street. Improperly or carelessly used, the patrol car can become a death trap. In an earlier chapter two police officers were trapped when they put an armed suspect in their car without a search. In similar situations, officers have given their adversaries an even better chance.

For example:

The two policemen were working in uniform and riding in a marked patrol car. Their assignment was general patrol, particularly to patrol a residential neighborhood plagued by car clouters and cat burglars. At 1:20 AM, it was still very hot, hot enough to be uncomfortable outside and barely comfortable inside the car even with the air conditioner on. The full moon and clear sky made driving without lights relatively easy. The green and white patrol car slowly cruised southbound, down the quiet residential street.

The officers saw the man simultaneously as he crossed the intersection almost a block ahead of them. The policemen turned west at the corner. Now the man was only 100 feet ahead and walking on the sidewalk on the south side of the street. Pulling up at the curb next to the casual stroller, the driving officer turned on the headlights, and quickly flicked on, then off, the overhead red light.

The man stopped immediately, then turned and waved in response to the officer's "Hi, where're you headed," as the car window was rolled down.

"Live around here?" asked the policeman.

"Close by," responded the man, now walking across the grass parkway to the patrol car. "I'm just out trying to get cool. It's hot and the air conditioner in the house broke down. I'm not sleepy anyway but when I get home I should be tired enough to get a good sleep."

"Where do you live?" The officer opened his shirt pocket and removed a pack of 3x5 cards. "What's your name?"

"Over on 62nd Street, I'm John White."

"Okay, what's the address?"

"1642" replied the man, kneeling now just outside the left front door so that he was looking up at the policeman behind the steering wheel writing on the F.I. card.

The dialogue could continue but it is irrelevant at this point. What is important is that the two policemen for any one of several reasons: apathy, over confidence, preoccupation, carelessness, laziness—take your choice—have placed themselves in a bad position. They are conducting a field interrogation while remaining in their car. In this case the subject has been allowed to remain outside, in a position ready to attack if the officers make a move to take him into custody or even request a want check on the radio.

What happened? The obvious of course. Both officers were shot by the neighborhood cat burglar. When the F.I. card was completed it was passed to the passenger officer. When that officer picked up the microphone to run a check for want and warrant the police vehicle became a death trap for one officer and the beginning of a life of intermittent pain and maimed hell for the other.

Both officers were shot because their approach from the start was improper. The officers had every advantage: training, physical fitness, weapons, darkness, mobility, the cover of their patrol car. The odds were more than two to one in their favor and they gave it all away.

The approach should have been made so the disadvantage was to the subject, not to the policemen. The time, place and circumstances permitted a pat down search for weapons and reasonable inquiry. But a proper pat-down search can hardly be done by officers sitting inside a police car while the subject remains outside. Also, it would seem that the legal right to make a pat-down search and inquiry is lost if the approach to the subject is made in a disinterested and relaxed manner.

If the officers had reacted properly the armed and dangerous ex-convict they stopped would possibly have gone back to the state penitentiary for violation of parole rather than to death row as a cop killer and there would have been one less, unnecessary police funeral in that city that year.

Police officers are at a disadvantage in approaching unknown or unresolved situations in the field. Police officers cannot approach everyone all the time with gun drawn and ready. I believe, however, the police officer must be allowed to draw his weapon if he knows the approaching situation portends violence or if he sincerely believes the situation has a potential for violence.

In many ways the police officer is at a greater disadvantage than the front line combat infantryman. The soldier on patrol can, and must, react quickly if a sudden and unexpected movement in the brush becomes suspicious. The soldier's instinctive response usually results in automatic weapons fire to destroy the bush and whatever was causing the suspicious movement—the enemy, the wind, or even an unfortunate friend in the wrong place at the wrong time. The police officer is not, and cannot be, allowed to use such deadly force on mere suspicion while he is on patrol in the street. The police officer's advantage lies in his mental and physical conditioning, training and equipment. None of these advantages should be given away through apathy, preoccupation or lazy carelessness while making an approach to an unknown or yet unresolved situation.

A method to measure and evaluate the quality of supervision and alertness in a police department may be accomplished by observation of the officer while he is on patrol in the street:

1. Traffic stop situations. Is the police car parked so that the officer's approach can be made in safety? Has the officer maintained a position of advantage?

2. Stance and position during a field interrogation or while issuing a traffic citation. Is the officer standing in a point of vantage? If there are two officers, have they eliminated a cross fire problem and have they precluded the chance for the

subject to attack them simultaneously? Does the officer remain alert and watchful, or does he turn his back while he completes the F.I. card or citation?

3. Are good search and handcuff procedures followed?

4. Are seating positions correct in the police car while transporting the prisoner(s)? There are a number of training texts that correctly describe acceptable and safe prisoner transportation seating arrangements in police cars. Yet, time after time, when police officer murder cases are reconstructed, it is found that prisoners were sitting in the rear alone with both officers in front; or the prisoner was seated in the rear behind the driving officer.

The subject of police officers disarmed and shot (not disarmed at gunpoint) must be discussed.

In the chapter on the proper use of handcuffs a case was mentioned of a detective who was disarmed and shot by a handcuffed prisoner being returned on a warrant of extradition. Carelessness by the officer was evident in that case. A review of the 1972, 1973, and 1974 FBI "Law Enforcement Officers Killed Summary" shows several instances of police officers disarmed and murdered. Most of these shootings happened during physical resistance to arrest and perhaps might be classed as unavoidable.

These cases, in which police officers were murdered after being disarmed primarily during an altercation, are mentioned only to alert law enforcement personnel that this type of police killing is increasing dramatically.

Another situation involves police officers who are shot with guns left in desks in police stations.

Chubby desk sergeants, chubbier watch commander lieutenants and tired old detectives would think twice before dropping their gun in the top desk drawer after arriving at work if they could have overheard a conversation I once had with a thrice convicted market bandit. I was told how he once escaped by taking a gun from a police station desk drawer and then putting three embarrassed policemen (that's right, the desk sergeant, the watch lieutenant, and the detective) in their own jail cell. He knew the best place to look. He mentally noted that they were *all* unarmed. Though he was handcuffed (in front) he only had to quietly open one desk. Having the gun, the rest was easy. His command to be unhandcuffed was obeyed, as was his order to the officers to lock themselves in the cell. The officers were fortunate that he limited his exploits to banditry and escape, not killing.

Taking a bad position, and "tombstone" courage, have too often unnecessarily cost the lives of police officers during problems related to barricaded and armed subjects.

Usually the confrontation is with an emotionally disturbed person who because of personal problems either real or imagined, has temporarily lost his, or her, sanity. If a weapon is available shooting is almost inevitable. Standard police tactics unfortunately often result in an uncoordinated and unsupervised gun battle between the subject and as many police officers available to respond. Too often, police officers at the scene, acting without established tactical plans or leadership, commit individual acts of heroism (tombstone courage) or inadvertently take poor positions of cover (taking a bad position). Both have resulted in unnecessary police fatalities. If the barricaded subject is an armed felon (or felons) proper strategy and tactics do not necessarily change. In most instances a wanted felon is easier to talk to than the temporarily mentally deranged citizen. Regardless of who the barricaded subject might be, the goal for the police remains the

162

same: to neutralize the situation without bloodshed.

Effective strategy and tactics have been established by departments with well trained, disciplined and equipped S.W.A.T. (Special Weapons And Tactics) or S.T.A.R. (Special Tactics And Response) teams. Special weapons and equipment may be used depending on the reaction of the barricaded subject. Proper response, initial perimeter, cover and containment tactics must be known and understood by *every* officer in the department. Supervisory and command response must follow immediately The specialists, S.W.A.T. or S.T.A.R., then take over the interior perimeter. Time is on the side of the police and the officers at the scene must have disciplined patience and be prepared to out-wait the subject, if possible. Of course, if the subject chooses to use firearms, then the force necessary to neutralize the situation must be used to avoid injury or death to innocent persons. The return fire by the police, however, should be controlled and the responsibility of the special teams. If an assault is deemed necessary it should be a last resort; and again, by trained and properly equipped specialists.

Law enforcement agencies which have *not* yet established S.W.A.T or S.T.A.R. teams should expect the following events to occur if a barricaded gunman situation erupts in their cities:

— Plan on your police officers (all of them) to respond quickly and react bravely—and individually;
— Plan on most of your police officers to take a bad position, i.e., poor positions of concealment and cover;
— Plan on the barricaded gunman to be eventually captured or killed;
— If you are lucky, plan to reward one or more of your officers with a Medal of Valor;
— If you are not quite so lucky, plan on a hospital visit to one or more of your officers who were shot during the episode (per-

haps by other police officers);

— If you are very unlucky, plan on a funeral.

In closing the "taking a bad position" subject I mention an act performed so often that its potential for injury and death for police officers is completely overlooked. It is done at least once, and usually a half dozen times a day, by patrol officers, investigators, or personnel assigned to security patrol.

The act I refer to is the position the officer takes when checking a door, knocking on a door, or ringing a doorbell to announce his or her presence. Invariably the officer will stand squarely in front of the door, or window; a position of great danger should a person on the other side decide to shoot. Do NOT stand in front of a door or a window. In a very recent case, two patrol officers stopped to make a Friday night security check of a dry cleaning establishment that had been burglarized three times, all on Friday nights, in the past two months. One officer went to the rear entrance, grasped the doorknob and shook the door. The officer was unaware the owner of the business had decided to remain inside the store all weekend to prevent another burglary. When the door rattled the startled owner believed the thief had returned and was attempting to force an entry. He fired two shots through the door with a .45 caliber automatic.

Fortunately the police officer did not die, but he spent almost two weeks in the Intensive Care ward of the County General Hospital.

I always discuss "taking a bad position" when I present my street survival lectures to police officers. I not only discuss the subject, but I walk to the classroom door and demonstrate how easy it is to accomplish the same objective, and eliminate any potential hazard, by standing to the side of the door, then reaching out and knocking with only my forearm and hand exposed. I tell the

164

class to start doing it this way now; here at the academy, at home, and even when you visit dear old mom. I advise them to start making this a habit. Don't stand facing the door when you knock or ring the bell. Eventually that habit might save your life.

Invariably, after my demonstration, there are a few muted chuckles. During the break the class humorist must demonstrate this newly learned safety technique to his peers prior to entering the men's room. But the humor is short lived after the break.

With the class reseated I tell them of a recent visit I made to a police department to talk to a group of young police officers. One of the officers was in a wheelchair. It was unreal to watch him. He had really mastered the art of moving about. He could make the thing do almost anything: forwards, backwards, turn on a dime.

Several months before, I was told he had responded to an unknown trouble call. Upon arriving at an old downtown hotel he was advised by the day manager that "weird" sounds were coming from room 402. Several of the guests had complained. The officer entered the elevator and rode up in the cage with the manager. As they approached the room they heard a muffled cry. The officer took the keys from the manager and waved him back. He walked to number 402 and put his ear to the door. Strange sounds indeed were coming from within. The policeman called out loudly. "Hey in there, are you O.K.?" Then he shouted, "police, open up," and knocked on the door. His fourth rap on the door coincided almost perfectly with the first of four shots that were fired through the door and into his midsection by a mentally disturbed and hallucinating alcoholic female.

As I said, he was unreal. I was amazed at how easily the young officer could move about in his motorized wheelchair by using only his right index finger and thumb. Those two digits, along with his neck and head, were the only nonparalyzed parts of his body.

tombstone courage   10

tombstone courage

10

Police officers have been described in various ways by many people, and usually the description is based on the personal contact or interaction the person has had with a police officer or a law enforcement agency. Police officers are said to be honest, firm, strong, friendly, kind, helpful, brave, etc. Unfortunately, we must admit at times the opposite is sometimes true. Undesirables do manage to become police officers and the majority of us suffer when improper conduct committed by a very small minority is brought to light.

Though variously described, police officers share a common trait —courage. It seems incredible to me that a young man or woman would even consider becoming a police officer without possessing the trait of courage. I suppose that somewhere, at some time, there might have been a cowardly police officer, but I doubt that once the trait of cowardice appeared the individual was able to remain in law enforcement for long.

The problem related to courage in law enforcement is a deadly phenomena that was for many years identified as "false courage." But "false" was inappropriate. A better choice we thought, could be illogical, fallacious, unsound or impractical. The word false as it was being referred to in this instance should not be construed to mean deceptive, or improper conduct. Then a good friend of law enforcement defined it perfectly—"tombstone courage."

The tombstone courage related here refers to the unnecessary risks and acts often committed by police officers in the line of duty. Unfortunately, these acts of courage are high on the list of proximate causes that lead to death or to serious injury of police officers throughout the world.

Many cases can be cited to typify this costly and unnecessary tragedy in law enforcement. Though I have not received detailed information in each case, it is not difficult to identify cases of tombstone courage in the summaries of the 1972, 1973, and 1974 issues of "Law Enforcement Officers Killed" published by the FBI Uniform Crime Reporting Program.

I am personally aware of the events that occurred in the following cases—events that occurred many years before the summaries were first printed by the FBI several years ago. Not much has changed. Police officers are still persons of great courage. Unforunately, many fine police officers did not combine their great courage with good judgment.

For example:

Several years ago a police officer on patrol observed a man dart out of a service alley behind a large shopping complex. When the man saw the police cruiser he ran forward waving frantically to the officer. The policeman stopped at the curb and was told by the man, an employee of an expensive men's clothing store, that on returning from a lunch break he'd seen a robbery in progress in the store as he started to walk through the partially opened rear door. He told the officer he saw a man pointing a gun at the back of his employer who was obviously being forced to open a wall safe.

The officer reacted quickly. He parked his car and transmitted the information via radio to his dispatcher. The dispatcher acknowledged immediately and alerted all police units in the vicinity. As the patrolman stepped out of his car he heard another patrol unit advise the dispatcher, "I'm six blocks east, will cover the front, ETA one minute." Then, according to witnesses, the police officer walked rapidly down the alley and into the rear of the store with his gun drawn. He was shot three times in the back and fatally wounded by the suspect who had hidden behind the rear door just before the officer entered.

The above incident occurred years ago in a Northwestern state. Recently I was told by a police officer in a Southeastern state that a policeman in his city was killed responding to a robbery in progress call. Again I hear the same story. The alarm, silent or reported by a citizen, the all units call, response by several officers, the first officer arrives and does not wait for backup. He enters and is shot to death by the bandits.

In retrospect, a careful analysis of these two cases reveal nothing much has changed. There is the same great courage of the officers as they unnecessarily exposed themselves and were killed. The frustration and sorrow of their brother officers—no change. The grief and tragic aftermath for their families—all the same. There are only two differences in the two cases; the locations of the incident, and the last names of the widows.

In another case:

Two heavily armed ex-convicts, paroled only one month before as "rehabilitated," entered a neighborhood supermarket late at night and a few minutes before closing time. They emphasized their demands in the classic style of the professional bandit: threats to "blow off your fucking heads," with sawed-off shotguns. The employees and a few remaining customers, except one whom the bandits did not see dart out a side door, were easily controlled. Several minutes later, while scooping out the cash from the registers, the robbers realized the market had been surrounded by police officers. They took cover by running upstairs to the manager's empty office on the second level.

As the officers entered the store they took cover. They were advised of the robbers' hiding place as the civilians scurried for safety. Intermittently, for the next twenty minutes, the sergeant in command called on the two men to throw down their guns and surrender. There was no response from the upper level office.

Then one patrolman, an officer known to be very aggressive and at times, a little too belligerent and abrasive, started up the stairs, revolver held ready in his right hand. The sergeant called out the man's name and gestured for him to return to his position of cover. Several policemen nearby heard the officer curse and mutter "those bastards don't scare me any, let's get this over with."

When the advancing policeman was seven steps up and six from the top, two simultaneous shotgun blasts from the manager's office reverberated loudly through the store.

The patrolmen on the store level watched in disbelief and horror as the almost headless body of the officer slowly tumbled down the stairs.

And in another, almost identical case:

174

Two uniformed officers were dispatched to a silent alarm robbery in progress call at a small all-night market. When they arrived they were told by an excited teenager that, "Two men are in the store with guns and are taking Mr. Gray's money."

As the officers were verifying the robbery on their radio and requesting backup units, a detective sergeant who had heard the call while returning to the station, arrived at the scene. The detective told the uniformed officers to cover front and rear then drew his two inch revolver and walked in the front door of the store alone. Several shots were heard and seconds later the two robbers ran from the store.

Almost immediately, upon command to do so, they threw down their guns and surrendered when confronted by one officer in good cover position behind his patrol car with a shotgun.

The detective, after taking only two steps inside the door, had been shot three times. He fell and died almost instantly.

I am certain that police officers everywhere would say that the four officers in these related incidents were men of exceptional courage. There is no question that a great deal of courage is required to walk into a place knowing that armed men could be committing a robbery, or to advance up a flight of stairs toward two trapped and heavily armed bandits.

Every year police officers throughout the world respond to calls that require the capture of armed criminals who are seen, then trapped in the places they are looting. Every year hundreds of police officers, because of their natural aggressiveness and courage, expose themselves unnecessarily to death and serious injury while responding to such calls. All of us have done it. Most of us have been lucky. None of us has been too smart.

During my lectures, many young officers have told me, "But, it's our duty to respond and capture the holdup men."

"True," is my response. "But by using good judgment and common sense. It's not cowardly to respond and take a position of cover; it's sensible to consider tactics to wait until the bandits exit, then force their surrender. If they begin to shoot, neutralize their capability to return fire."

"But," a member of the class asks, "What about people inside, shouldn't we go in and help them?"

"That's the primary reason for our response, to help them. More so perhaps than to capture the bandits. But an immediate unplanned entry is not necessarily the best method to aid the trapped citizens. It might very well be the worst possible method. There would be exceptions, of course, since every case is different. That's why tactical plans for felony in progress calls must be flexible. But there must be established basic plans.

"Remember, all of the policemen in the stories just related went in and all were killed—and that's not the only time that has happened."

"But," the young officer replies, "if you don't go in you could be setting up a hostage situation. If the stickup men are trapped inside, they will use the civilians in the store as hostages."

"Could be," I reply. "It's happened. But you shouldn't plan on closing out a hostage scene by rushing inside. If you do, make up a contingency plan for mass funerals, and not just for the suspects, but perhaps for bystanders, the hostages, and even yours. There's a lot of new thinking now on tactics in a hostage situation, but this is neither the time nor the place to discuss that subject."

176

"Remember another thing," I tell the class. "If you do go in, you have a tremendous disadvantage. You can be immediately identified. If the store, or let's say a bank, is crowded, how do you identify the holdup man as quickly as he'll be able to identify you? Do you think he'll be standing in an exposed position? Think about it. The best way is to establish a perimeter to preclude the subject's escape. Then wait for him or them to come out and make the apprehension. Too many courageous policemen have been killed trying to do it on their own or by just not following well planned tactics. I'm aware of a situation where two policemen, entering one at a time and several minutes apart at a robbery in progress situation, were disarmed by the holdup men. No, they weren't killed but after it was all over they had to write reports on why it happened. Pride and ego sure gets shattered in a case like that."

Now, two classics to close the discussion on tombstone courage.

Several years ago I was invited to make a survival presentation at an in-service training seminar at Fox Hollow Falls, a small rural community in the northeast corner of the state. The seminar was attended by many small town police officers, rural county sheriffs and their deputies. After my three-hour lecture, I was invited to have lunch with one of the veteran local deputies. I was told an interesting and one of my most unforgettable stories.

In these small communities in "cow counties" it was not uncommon for one lonely patrolman to be the only law enforcement officer on duty at any one time within a large geographic area. When things had to be done, it was by necessity a one-man job; traffic stops, building checks, suspicious incidents or whatever.

Traditionally then, but actually as a matter of availability, there were no calls made for backup units or assistance except in cases of dire emergency. I was told the attitude of the rural police officer was that if you couldn't handle an arrest or a little break-in by yourself, you weren't fit to be a lawman.

Then, about a year before my visit, the new bridge and the interstate were completed. Times had changed. Fox Hollow Falls was taking on the air of a resort community. As the town grew, so did the police department, the sheriff's office, traffic congestion, and the crime rate. Younger and better trained men were being employed in both departments and were doing things that the "old timers" scoffed at. One tactic used by the newcomers was the request for backup when an officer believed the situation "might" warrant a second patrolman at the scene. The veterans termed this to be "chicken" and although they responded when asked to assist, they never would embarrass themselves by asking for assistance in their "routine cases." They had, after all, handled things for years without ever asking for a backup.

Then it happened. It happened to an old timer named Casey. Casey had been around a long time, according to my story telling lunch partner. Casey's family was one of the original settlers in the valley. As a boy, I was told, Casey used to take out food scraps and had made a pet out of the fox in the hollow at the falls. Initially on horseback, then by car, Casey had patrolled the Fox Hollow Falls area for over thirty years.

About six months earlier, the story continued, Casey was on patrol. At about 4:30 AM he happened on a car with a warm hood parked behind Art Johnson's new sporting goods store. Silently scoffing at the thought of requesting a backup, Casey quietly walked to the corner of the building and peered inside. Almost immediately, he saw the thin beam of light searching through a display case in the center of the store. Now Casey gave

178

a second thought to a call for backup. But then he remembered those roll call discussions and how he'd "put down" the new men when they discussed cover in entry procedures during a burglary in progress situation. The hell with it, thought Casey, if he couldn't take care of the burglar by himself, he ought to pull the pin. Mostly though, he silently admitted, he could hardly concede to the younger officers that a backup was what he really wanted, right now.

Cautiously, Casey stepped inside the jimmied door, quickly turned on his five-cell flashlight and aimed his six inch revolver at the light glowing on the cash register. Casey's call identifying himself and for the burglar to surrender echoed simultaneously with the shot fired by the thief. Both Casey and the burglar were lucky. The thief had an automatic. His first shot smashed Casey's flashlight and numbed his left hand and arm to the elbow. Then the gun jammed. Casey's revolver, however, worked very well. All six shots fired. Every one was a near miss. Before the thunderous blast of the old six shooter died down, the uninjured suspect was screaming for surrender from behind the smashed showcase. Casey had himself a burglar without even using the backup.

Casey is a fine lawman, and a man of great courage. He knows he was indeed lucky that night when he found the burglar in Johnson's sporting goods store. Now, while on patrol, old Casey calls for a backup when he feels the situation demands it. And he's not ashamed to admit it.

He told me so while we had lunch together after my lecture in Fox Hollow Falls.

Another case of tombstone courage, another classic: a true story that occurred over twenty years ago.

The subject, a young police officer, had just been appointed sergeant. Established personnel policy required his automatic transfer to a patrol division located far from the detective division he had worked for the past several years.

Perhaps this young man had become a sergeant too soon or perhaps the department had not yet learned to properly train their field supervisors for what has been termed the most difficult of all promotions, the transition of policeman to sergeant.

The neophyte sergeant was apprehensive, no doubt about it. The first year on the job had been in uniform, in a patrol car and walking a beat. Then a transfer to a detective division. A two-year recall to active duty in the Navy, and on returning, another year as an investigator, had far removed him from the trials and tribulations of the world of the street patrolman.

The patrol division of his new assignment had a reputation. Tough neighborhood and tough cops. Tough old cops not easily led by new, young probationary sergeants. When the promotion and transfer list had been printed, a hardnosed old lieutenant had called and gruffly advised him to show up at 2300 hours, suited up and ready to handle the morning watch roll call.

That night in the huge room on the second floor of the old brick police station, the sergeant completed roll call and read teletypes. At 11:45 PM he dismissed his non-commital charge to their radio cars in the parking lot below. It would not be wise, he thought, to pull an inspection this night. Besides, he should first check the department manual to make sure he had properly placed the equipment carried on his own Sam Browne belt.

Several nights later he had definitely made up his mind. It stood to reason, he thought, that in order to prove his worth he must show his men he had the same quality of courage they all surely

180

must have. The proof was in the doing. Talking about it would fall on deaf ears with this group, he was convinced.

So the young sergeant set out to establish himself as "one of the men." Totally confused as to his primary responsibility, supervision, he proceeded to make car stops, recover stolen autos, and apprehend burglars. All this while riding solo. Sergeants, supposedly restricted to supervising responsibilities, rode alone in a patrol division that assigned patrolmen in pairs, from dusk to dawn, for their protection.

One morning about a month later, at approximately 3:00 AM, the patrolmen in the division were alerted by their dispatcher— "All units and 3 Adam 33, an ambulance shooting, 4567 West Vermont, 3 Adam 33, Code 3."

The sergeant was elated. He was only 3 blocks east of the location. An ambulance shooting Code 3. It had to be a really hot call, maybe even a homicide. He could easily get there first, and perhaps apprehend the suspect, or at least put out a description before the first patrol car could arrive. His men would be convinced he had the guts to move in on a hot call by himself.

As he pulled up in front of the house and got out of his cruiser, the sergeant heard the wail of a siren in the distance. Glancing quickly to the west, he saw flashing red lights coming over the brow of a hill. That would be 3 Adam 33 he knew, but they were still 60 seconds or more away. Why wait? He could have it all wrapped up before they could park their car, get out and enter the house.

He could see several lights on in the old two-story frame home as he ran up the front steps. Pounding loudly on the door, the sergeant was about to shout for the third time, "Police Officer, open up" when the door suddenly opened.

A form of paralysis set in. Standing in front of the sergeant, almost filling the doorway, was a huge, half-naked man. He was at least six foot six and close to 250 pounds. No fat. The man was also holding a very large shotgun.

In a split second, several fleeting thoughts raced through the sergeant's mind: the man holding the shotgun was so big that he probably could kill him without even using the gun . . . he wished the officers in unit 3 Adam 33 were here with him, now . . . he might never become a lieutenant . . . he had made one or more tactical errors . . . if he lived he would never commit those errors again.

Then the big man moved and spoke. Holding out the shotgun, he told the sergeant, "Here, I've just killed my wife. Arrest me."

Like Casey in Fox Hollow Falls, the young sergeant realizes how lucky he was. He knows that Casey and he are but two of the countless hundreds of police officers who have been fortunate enough to have committed a fatal error without becoming a fatality.

Today, the young sergeant is an old chief who uses the story to emphasize the tactical errors created by tombstone courage. In this incident, the one just related, it was a near personal tragedy. I was not a courageous hero that morning when I jumped the ambulance shooting call assigned to 3 Adam 33. I was a damned fool!

a premonition 11

a premonition 11

The following conversation was recorded during an early morning seminar held in the Spring of 1974. Chiefs of police, several sheriffs, and high-ranking police command officers from a five-state region were in attendance.

The seminar topic was, "Contemporary Personnel Issues in Law Enforcement." The subject under discussion prior to the coffee break had been, "Women in Police." There is background noise as the meeting continues after the break: the coffee service cart being wheeled out of the room, and the voices of several of the participants as they take their chairs at the conference table.

Chief S. A.:

". . . and I'm still having a problem converting over to proper titles. I learned to say councilperson real quick, particularly after we had three women elected to our council two months ago. I'm sort of getting used to police officer or policewoman, instead of patrolman, but eliminating gender is a difficult habit to change after all these years."

Chief R. B.:

"Yeah I know. I keep thinking my department has made the switch. But I got a few old holdouts who would rather fight than switch. One of my salty old-timers who was writing up a traffic accident report last week asked one of our female officers how to properly refer to a manhole cover."

Chief J. R.:

"Talk about salty response, I went to a meeting last month up North. One of the Chiefs up there is obviously against using women. He said when the Vikings started a game with a female linebacker, he would start using women on patrol."

(Laughter and a partly unintelligible question follows.)

". . . Do you think about . . . report?"

Chief S. L.:

"I'll tell you what I think of that report, the one on 'Women in Police'—bullshit. That's what I think, bullshit! It's just like the rest of their reports. Ever notice who researches, conducts and evaluates their projects? Same kind of people. What they should do is get some experienced police chiefs who have really proven

188

themselves as top-grade administrators. Instead, their research and evaluation is done by a couple of chiefs who couldn't hack it, or got canned, and a couple of those phony Ph.D.'s who have been stroking the LEAA moneypot for the past five years. For Christ's sakes, anybody can make a report sound good if you get your own evaluators. That's about like the defense and prosecution each picking a psychiatrist in a murder trial and then pretending not to know how the shrinks will testify."

Chief G. W.:

"Yeah, or the KKK doing an evaluation entitled, "A Critical Analysis of Lynching at Midnight in Relation to Community Crime Prevention."

Chief L. H.:

"Come on, George, lay off us rednecks. Remember, if you Yankees hadn't of mistreated Mr. Miranda and Mrs. Mapp, we all wouldn't be messed up like we are."

Chief C. M.:

"Okay. Okay. Let's get back on the track. We're supposed to be here to try and resolve the problems, not aggravate them. What about you, Lou? We've heard you are training women now. How are you handling the problem? Do you have any of your women out on patrol yet?"

Chief L. C.:

"No, Charlie, not yet. But I guess it's coming and I won't be able to think of any more excuses to put it off. Frankly, the thought of those little girls out on the street alone scares me to death. I know some of you think you've solved the problem by taking the tough guy approach. You've just said the hell with it, dressed up some women in patrolmen uniforms and then thrown them out in the street on their own. I suppose you think that's some form of retribution against a change in the system you know you can't beat. Either that or you're waiting for one of them to get knocked on their can so you can say I told you so.

"Well, I don't think that's right. Besides, I think you're setting yourself up for a real problem when one of them eventually gets hurt, and one will someday, believe me. What I'm going to do is give every one of them the best damn training available and turn them loose when my watch commanders say they're ready.

"If women are supposed to hit the street as patrol officers, then so be it. But I admit it scares the hell out of me. I just can't help worrying about it."

Authors Note: It is neither necessary nor important to identify, for the usual reasons, those present and speaking at this seminar. What is important is not so much what was said or how it was said, but the obvious concern of the speakers. Regardless of their apparent differences in expressing their views of women on police patrol, I cannot help but believe that the oratorical bravado of some of those chiefs present (and many others whom I have heard that were not) was in fact, deep seated concern and anxiety in disguise. All of them I believe, not just one but all of them, had a premonition.

The ending of the story that follows is fiction; at least it is as of this writing.

The reader will probably question why this incident is included in a book of factual cases. The story, I believe, is relevant on three counts. First, by now the reader will recognize the several classic deadly errors, committed on the street, which have been the causes in the deaths of many hundreds of fine police officers. Several of those deadly errors should be easily recognized and identified in this story. Although they probably would not readily admit the allegation, all "working" police officers have committed one or more of the deadly errors. Most of us have just been lucky up to now. Recognizing the errors is one thing; admitting them and then remaining alert is another.

Second, this story might well be controversial and upset many police officers, particularly women police officers. If the reader becomes uneasy and perturbed with the story but retains the message, then I have achieved the desired result.

Third, I have said that the ending of the story is fictitious. Maybe by the time the readers turn these pages it will not be fiction at all. I too, have a premonition.

Publisher's Note: This story, including the foreword and preface, was written prior to the incident that occurred in September, 1974 when the first patrolwoman in the history of U.S. law enforcement was shot and killed in the line of duty while pursuing robbery suspects in Washington, D.C.

Part One

Officer John MacReadie picked up the microphone as the dark blue and white squad car braked to a stop in the police headquarters parking lot.

"2 Young 34, end of watch."

The dispatcher's voice replied crisply, "2 Young 34 Roger, Officer Moore to report to 2 Adam 30 in the watch commander's office."

MacReadie responded, "Roger," replaced the mike on the dashboard clip and turned towards his partner. "What's that all about, or can I guess?"

"Don't know, but there's one way to find out."

Officer Moore pushed in the headlight switch, then turned off and removed the ignition key.

"I'll turn in the keys and see what the sergeant wants me for. You check in the shotgun and paperwork, okay?"

"Good enough," resonded MacReadie. "We're all caught up on our reports. I'll turn in the DFAR and FI cards, then I'm going to cut out."

"Right, see you tomorrow Mac."

Patrol Officer Mary Beth Moore walked across the lot sidestepping the small puddles of black ice formed in the craters of the old asphalt parking area. Dangerous damn stuff, she mumbled to herself, then thinking back to about six months ago she remembered her first fatal traffic accident call was the result of the treacherous and invisible black ice. Field Training Officer Roger Steele had been with her that night when they were one of the two units assigned to back up an AI car that had received an "ambulance traffic, Code 3," on the 23rd Avenue curve at Broadway. The scene of scattered wreckage made Mary think of a kind of midnight demolition derby. Even the fans were there, she thought as she pushed her way through the gathering crowd of curious onlookers. Apparently a big new four-wheel drive station wagon had hit some black ice on the curve, skidded out of control into oncoming traffic, ricocheted off a pickup loaded with firewood, uprooted the northwest corner light pole, decapitating a pedestrian in the process, and then still at high speed, slid broadside into a small oncoming sports car. As Mary walked through the wreckage, she glanced at a corpseless head lying like a centerpiece among a setting of splintered chromium strips and shards of glass. The ambulance crew had carefully covered the corpse but in their frantic attempts to save the mangled and crushed survivors, had missed the severed head.

Then Mary became upset, really upset. But not at the gruesome evidence. The division traffic sergeant in charge, noting Mary's arrival ordered her to, "Move on up the street and direct traffic out of the number 1 and number 2 lanes Miss Moore. I don't want you puking all over the street in public view."

Mary diverted traffic as she was told but was piqued because she knew she was ordered off because she was "Miss Moore," rather than "Officer Moore." Someday, she thought, I'll be accepted as well as any of the men on the beat. But how to achieve that recognition?

Now, a "veteran" of one year, Mary had been more or less accepted as a good policewoman. She knew she was head and shoulders above her peers, the other women assigned to patrol. But on occasion, by the comments, the looks, and the actions of the men, she was still being reminded that she was a woman in a man's profession. At least three times now, on her last series of monthly probationary evaluation reports, she had been counseled by her team sergeant about becoming too uptight on the subject.

"Let it come, Moore, let it come." The sergeant pointed a pencil at her as he leaned forward in his chair. "Dammit," he growled, "You try too hard. What the hell you want to be anyway, Amy Prentiss in one year?"

"No sir," she responded, trying hard to remain composed, "I just want to be a good police officer, but not necessarily a woman in a police uniform."

"Oh crap, Moore, you are, you are." The sergeant threw down his pencil and shook his head. "You are, you know, you're a good police officer. You've earned that by hard work. But you're going to screw it up by being too eager. As far as being a woman is concerned, accept the fact you are. It's too late to change now."

Part Two

Mary walked into the police building and shook her head to no one in particular as she recalled that one-sided conversation with her sergeant. *Wonder what he wants now? I hope it's about that new assignment the Chief promised.* First though, she would take a few minutes to freshen up and check her appearance.

Turning left, Mary walked a short distance, then paused as she started to enter the locker room. She frowned, then muttered in

194

silent indignation as she read the chauvinistic graffitti sprawled on the door. Just below the "Policewomen Only" sign, there had been printed in large red block letters, "Dickless Tracys." One of her male counterparts, without doubt.

Mary stiff armed the door and walked in. She hung her heavy jacket in her locker and began to think of the forthcoming meeting with her sergeant. By the time she had washed up, the bigoted communique on the door had been dismissed from her conscious thoughts.

Next she stopped before the full length mirror that hung on the wall of the small room. She checked right side, left, then front again. *Not bad if I say so myself,* she mused, then silently described herself in jargon known by police officers throughout the land. *Female, Cauc, 24, five nine and one-half.* She paused, then continued mentally with her own physical characterization; *142, brown, hazel, and wearing the uniform of a police officer.* "Of a police patrol officer," she said aloud to herself.

She looked up, then down. She pulled the big chromium buckle of her Sam Browne belt a bit to the right. Then she pressed the release on the clam shell and removed the 4 inch .38 caliber revolver from its well-polished holster. Clean, no dust. She opened the chamber, closed it and reseated the gun. Glancing at her badge she smiled. That was the part of her uniform she was most proud of and it was kept gleaming at all times.

Stepping forward, she peered more closely at her reflection. A bit husky perhaps? Well, Barney didn't seem to mind at all. Thinking of Barney, she smiled. What Barney thought was becoming increasingly important to her these days. Mary chuckled, then as she recalled an earlier arrest she and MacReadie had made of an enraged whore with dyed gold hair. Mary remembered the huge blue ribbon looped through the pompadour and thought facetiously that the woman must have matriculated at the university located in Berkeley. The woman was high on dexies and wine at the time, and had just emasculated her ex-pimp boyfriend with a six-inch switchblade knife. The arrest was made more difficult as it was done in an old apartment house on a hardwood floor slippery with the blood of the unconscious eunuch. During the inevitable struggle, the prostitute had called Mary a "He-she," and later, during the booking process, had called her a lesbian. Barney would have most certainly disagreed she knew, particularly with the allegation that she might be a lesbian.

Part Three

Mary pushed open the locker room door, scowled again as she saw the spiteful red-lettered sign, then began walking toward the west end of the building. As she reached for a hallway door it opened, and two policemen started through as Mary stepped into the corridor. A patrolman, the oldest, stepped back and held the door open for her.

"I can handle a door," she snapped. Then remembering the discussion during a meeting with the chief two weeks ago, she quickly added, "but thanks." As she walked down the long hallway toward the watch commander's and sergeant's office she recalled that particular meeting.

The chief had scheduled one of his quarterly roundtable discussions two weeks ago last Tuesday. This time, however, rather than with the usual mixed group of 6 to 10 officers, he had set it up for policewomen only. All 12 of them. There had been the usual scuttlebutt prior to the meeting and the expected verbal barbs from some of the patrolmen.

196

Was the chief finally going to let them go out on patrol alone? Mary was sure that's what he would say. She knew that some of the women were still hesitant and wanted to stay with their male partners, but Mary didn't want to consider anything except a policy change that would schedule her to a patrol unit—solo!

Actually, the department had employed policewomen for over five years, but their assignments were mostly those traditionally meted out to female officers: juvenile runaways, juvenile counseling, front desk receptionists, records, and communications dispatch.

Then the present chief had come aboard last year and things began to change. "Police officers do police work," he had said. Very shortly thereafter, Mary heard for the first time about the increase in the "P.F.P." the Pucker Factor Parameters. It was discussed in particular by an extremely nervous group of veteran officers whom Mary and her friends had already concluded were on some kind of full-pay retirement status. At least they appeared to work as if already retired.

Within a month after the new chief's first command staff meeting, all sworn positions behind typewriters, in records, the property room and in dispatch had disappeared. Civilians were replacing those police officers who for years had languished without complaint in non-productive desk jobs.

These officers were now being reassigned to field duty—out on the street. Before the chief's third month had begun there was a rash of premature and unexpected resignations and early retirements. And the position of Assistant Chief was eliminated, much to the silent glee of all but one, the captain, who had since time immemorial it seemed, held that prestigious but administratively archaic position. "Captain Super Clerk" as he was unaffectionately known, had not ventured into the field from behind his desk for over ten years. Seven months after the new chief's arrival the captain announced his resignation. In an obsequious memo posted throughout the department by himself, he declared his decision to leave was due to the unfortunate changes in the public's attitude towards the modern day policeman on the street. "How he would've known that," a veteran robbery sergeant declared solemnly, "is going to be the big mystery case of the year that we'll probably never be able to solve."

New and aggressive nationwide recruiting efforts, including a two-year college requirement, had attracted hundreds of applicants to the department. The rookie class of the past Spring was thirty-two strong, including seven young women, one of whom was Mary Beth Moore. Today, the women of the department worked major case investigations, Training Division, Intelligence Division, and patrol. But those in patrol rode with a male partner, while the men patrolled their beats in one-man cars.

Initially the chief had justified (or rationalized, Mary thought) his reason for not permitting the women to patrol alone. "They must be available if they're suddenly needed for a special problem," he had said at a departmental meeting early in the year. "If they're assigned to a patrol car alone one of our women could be tied up on a traffic accident, for instance, just when we need her for a special job. If she's with a partner we can leave the patrolman at the scene and have the policewoman respond where we need her. When we get more women, I'll think about cutting them loose on patrol alone."

And that's the way it had been for Mary's entire year on the job. For at least 9 of those 12 months she had been waiting impatiently for a solo assignment to patrol.

The meeting between the chief and his policewomen was a good one. During his almost 30 years on the job, the chief had been in nearly every kind of an action assignment and had picked up two degrees enroute. He could tell war stories that made sense, and on this occasion told two of them to cut the inevitable tension that exists in a room when one person, the speaker, has twice as much time on the job as the other twelve put together.

After a short coffee break the chief began to discuss department policy, particularly that oriented to the patrol function. When he reviewed the Use of Force policy, Mary was sure: *it's coming,* she thought. *He wouldn't have brought that up if he wasn't going to turn us loose.* And she was right.

"I've decided that it's time that you, those of you who are ready, can be assigned to a Zebra unit and go out on patrol on your own. I'll admit now that my concern over your safety has delayed this policy change. Other than that, I have no reason or excuse for that delay except perhaps some kind of misguided pater nalism."

Mary's mind raced with excitement and anticipation. Her eyes stung with emotion. *A strong man,* she thought. *At least he has the courage to admit why he'd backed off. I wish he could've been my watch commander rather than old Lt. Stone.*

The chief continued talking slowly, more slowly than usual, Mary thought. Then she was disturbed for a moment when she realized the chief was apprehensive about making his pronounce-ment. *Don't worry chief,* Mary told him silently. *I'll do you a hell of a job and bust as many or more stickup men and burglars than the best patrolmen we have.*

"If I've heard of any complaints about your work as female officers, and I have," the chief paused, "there is but one that concerns me. You, most of you, are trying too hard to prove you are the same as the men. Well you aren't." He looked down the circle of impassive but attentive faces.

"I can tell some of you don't like me saying that. I don't want to waste your time and mine going into why you are different, but you are and you know it. But that doesn't mean you can't go out and be good cops. In this department, if you don't cut it, you're out. Same as the men. It's as simple as that. Just do your job and it will all fall into place. If you try too hard you can make a mistake and fall on your face. I'm not trying to be poetic. I just don't want to end up planting you, or any other police officer in this department, in the local cemetery. God knows I've gone to enough police funerals."

Mary looked out of the corner of her eye at the other women in the room. He was making his point. One of her friends had visibly shuddered when the chief had said the word, "planted."

He sipped on his coffee, moved his chair back and continued. "And another thing." Now he leaned over the table and spoke more quickly. "Doing your job right is one thing, staying a lady is another. They can mix. You don't have to act and talk like a man to be a good police officer. I think the biggest gripe I have against this women's lib thing is the number of garbage mouthed, loud talking and overbearing women it has spawned. I guess I'm old fashioned about it. Hell, I don't guess, I know I am. Old fashioned, you know, is now defined as male chauvinism by the libbers. I'll go along with equal rights for women and a little silent cussing now and then, or even a shot of out-loud cussing at the right time. But there's a time and a place for everything, for both men and women."

The chief got up and walked to the coffee table. "You know," he said, refilling his cup, "you can act like a lady and still be a good police officer. That's your challenge. That's your real challenge and I don't think some of the policewomen of America have

200

realized that yet. We say we want our male officers to be gentlemen, don't we? That doesn't mean we want them to act like Caspar Milquetoast. I know keeping your cool on the street is hard to do today, maybe even harder than it was for me 25 years ago.

But that's no reason you can't act and talk like a lady, and still do the job. If the men in this department or the people on the street treat you like a lady, don't resent it, appreciate it."

He looked at them all again. One by one, it seemed to Mary. "I'll close now," he said, "and give you a chance to talk. I want you all to know I sincerely believe you're good police officers. If you weren't, you wouldn't be here with me now. Don't try to prove the point by getting hurt."

There was a brief question and answer period when the chief had finished. Mary took a deep breath and asked the last question of the day. "How soon, sir? How soon can we start?"

"Very soon, Mary. I'll pass the word through Deputy Chief Coleman today. It should be within a week or two. He'll have to make some deployment schedule changes."

The chief stood to leave, then readdressed the group. "I have something to say that might give you some insight on how I feel about all this. About our discussion today. If I didn't give a damn about you I would've had you out on the street alone months ago. But I do care, and not just for the obvious personal reason. But it's one we all do think about. All of the chiefs. No chief has lost a woman police officer yet. None of us wants to be first, but one of us has to be. All of us live with that terrible premonition. I'm no exception. Be careful and above all stay alert."

The moment the chief left the room it was filled with a buzz of conversation; some elated, some contemplative, and some concerned. Mary was unusually quiet and thoughtful. A premonition, he'd said. She'd heard that before, both recently and long before.

Part Four

Mary, recalling the chief's words as she walked down the hall, tried to remember when she had first heard the words, "I have a premonition." The thought drew a blank.

The two signs above the door said, "Watch Commander" and "Team Sergeants." As Mary walked into the office, an inner door opened and Sgt. Matthews appeared. He stopped and turned towards the figure standing behind the desk in the lieutenant's office. Mary heard Lt. Stone bellow at his sergeant, "I know that's what the chief wants and I know that's what we'll do, but that doesn't mean I got to like it. I gotta feeling, I tell you, the damn thing worries the hell outta me."

Sgt. Matthews backed up as the bulky figure of the lieutenant advanced on him, filling the doorway. Lt. Stone stopped as he saw Mary standing in front of the sergeant's desk. He opened and closed his mouth like a large-mouth bass gasping for air, but nothing came out. Then he shook his head, turned, and slammed the door.

Jesus, Mary thought to herself, *another one with some kind of premonition?* Strange about Lt. Stone, she thought, the old bear really likes me. I know that for sure. At times he was quiet, kind and helpful. But those were the times, she knew, when she was keeping herself in a "woman's proper place." But now the plan to put women in patrol cars, and particularly alone, had just been too much for the veteran traditionalist. Her thoughts were interrupted as she watched Sgt. Matthews sit down, put both hands to his temple for a moment and shake his head. Then he looked up and spoke to her.

"How'd it go tonight, Moore?"

"Okay, Sarge. No problems. Sort of a routine night."

"Yeah. Well maybe your routine will change a bit from now on. Tomorrow night you're 2 Zebra 22. But I guess that's what you've been wanting all along, right?"

Mary hoped she wasn't blushing, but it was no use. She could feel the warm flush rising in her cheeks. She would be the first woman in the department to be on patrol by herself.

"Thanks Sergeant." She could hear the lieutenant slamming drawers in the next room and wanted to get out of the office before he emerged from his cave to say what she knew he had wanted to say a few minutes before.

"I'll see you tomorrow night at roll call. Is that it?"

"No, and no," replied Matthews. "No, you won't see me tomorrow night at roll call, and no, that's not it." The sergeant glanced back at the door behind her, lowered his voice, and said, "I have to make a speech at West High tomorrow night. But I'll be back before end of watch. The lieutenant will handle roll call. That ought to be something to see and hear when he reads roll call and assigns you to a one-man car . . ."

Mary coughed.

"Aaaawwww, well, what the hell do we call it now? A one-woman car?"

"How about a Zebra unit, Sergeant?" said Mary, "that's the terminology that's used to identify a patrol unit with one . . ."

"Okay, okay, I know, I know, a Zebra unit. Now hear this also, Moore, loud and clear. I might as well be honest with you, I don't feel like the lieutenant does about all this, not quite. But your performance in the field is going to be watched. I got my orders." Matthews made the baseball "out" sign with his right hand, thumb pointed to the door of the lieutenant's office. "So don't expect any favors. And don't get so excited about it you'll foul up on your calls."

Mary thought of several replies that she would have liked to have made, but held back and said only, "I'll be okay, Sarge. I'm ready now and have been for over a half a year. As for feeling excited, I guess that got worn out waiting for this assignment to come."

"Yeah, but you have to admit it's different."

"Different?"

"Yeah, dammit, different. It's just different. Be on time tomorrow night, okay."

"Goodnight, Sergeant."

While driving home, Mary recalled her conversation with Sergeant Matthews, and the one she had overheard between him and Lieutenant Stone. I guess they're right in a way, she thought, there will always be some difference. Then she shook her head. But not out on the street. That definitely would not be different. Mary was determined that she would meet or exceed the performance of the rest of the troops. Someday, she pledged to herself, Lieutenant Stone, Sergeant Matthews, and the Chief would be forced to attest to that fact.

Part Five

Mary was in bed by 3:30 AM and as was her habit, read for awhile before going to sleep. She read two more chapters of Joe Wambaugh's latest book, muttering to herself about the strange technicalities of the law; guilt was not a factor in that case but the trial had lasted for years. Then she put the book on the night-stand and turned out the light. The best way to fall asleep was to mentally plan for tomorrow, or really she thought, the rest of her day, as it was already more than four hours into "tomorrow." It was her mother's birthday and Mary and her sister would visit, each bringing a remembrance. If it hadn't been for the birthday, she would have seen Barney and the team off at the airport.

She closed her eyes and thought of Barney, then smiled and hugged her pillow. He was really some kind of a guy. She was happy with him, very happy, and loved him very much. Barney had been her first real love and they had spent several wonderful nights together during the past several months after meeting on a ski-lift the day before Christmas Eve. Although it was not yet a subject for serious and extended discussion, both knew that they would most probably be married in the not-too-distant future.

Recently however, problems had come to the fore regarding her occupation as a police officer. Barney was back-up quarterback for the professional football team representing the greater metro-politan area of which Mary's city was the largest suburb. Barney,

205

a unanimous choice for All-American two years ago, had also been close to the top in the balloting for the Heisman trophy. This season he was getting considerably more playing time than he had during his rookie year as eleven years of being sacked several times each Sunday during the season was beginning to catch up with the team's twelve year veteran quarterback and offensive leader.

Barney wanted Mary out of police work and was becoming more adamant on the subject. He could easily support the two of them financially. He told her so as he promised his love forever.

One night, just a week earlier, while sitting in front of a blazing fire at their favorite retreat, Mary replied in response to his insistent request. "No, Barney, not yet. I'm just not ready to quit yet. And if I left now, it would seem just like that to me—quitting. I know I'll probably leave the department someday, particularly if we stay together. And I truly want us to stay together. A year ago, before we met, I wouldn't· have given a moment's thought of leaving the department. It was my life, and I had made up my mind. I was going to become chief of detectives some day or know the reason why."

She laughed, then became serious once more as she watched Barney shake his head in disbelief. "I'll do it when I feel it's the right time. Please be patient, Barney. If I did leave the department now, it might cause a fatal rift between us."

Barney leaned back, sighed heavily, and closed his eyes. "Okay, I'll try to understand. But I'll be honest with you, too. It scares me. You just mentioned a 'fatal' rift. When you said that, it made me jump. I don't like that word—fatal. I didn't want to think about it or even mention it, but when you said that it brought back a memory I've been trying to push out of my mind for a long time, particularly since I met you.".Barney paused and took a deep breath.

"One of my best buddies. We played three years together in high school, then we both went to State on a scholarship. Jake was an All-State running back in high school and second team All-Conference in his sophomore year at State. He was really fantastic. He had some kind of a record going for him that was the envy of every running back in the league. He had never fumbled. We realized this when he was a senior in high school and some reporter started to pick up on it. Even at State, in our freshman year and in our second year, he never fumbled the ball. I was supposed to be a pretty good quarterback and I can remember fumbling a couple of times, but he never did. He used to say to me, 'Hell, Barney, I can't afford to fumble. That could be a fatal error in any game.'"

Barney got up, walked to the fireplace, pulled back the screen and started stirring the glowing embers with a poker. He placed two pine logs on the grate and closed the screen. As he stood up the wood burst into crackling flames.

"Yeah, that's what he said alright. I remember it clear as day. I don't want to, but I do. He said, 'a fatal error.' Anyway, in the very first game in our junior year a big linebacker from Alabama did a thing on Jake's knee. He cracked him real hard as Jake broke into the secondary on a trap play. He caught him just right. Just right for the linebacker, but just wrong for Jake. It was about as bad a knee injury as you can get. A year later, he dropped out of school to support his family and got a job in the big city as a policeman. We still visited as he helped coach the freshman backs—they idolized Jake, and he kept going to class parttime. He said he needed that degree in order to pass the promotional exams he'd be taking in the future.

"He really loved that job, just like you do, I guess. Then a year and a half later he was dead. He was shot and killed making what he thought was a routine traffic stop on a stop sign violator. A couple of goofy speed-freaks in a stolen car blew him to pieces. Knowing Jake as I do—as I did, I know what he would've said, and that's what haunts me. I just can't get it out of my mind. I don't mean to be facetious, not about something like this, but I know exactly what he would've said: 'I guess I finally fumbled, Barney. I told you that could be a fatal error in any game.'"

Barney stopped, and shook his head. "The game of life," he said. "What a waste." Then he turned around and poked at the fire again. Mary realized that his voice had become very low and husky with emotion.

"I'm sorry Barney," she said. "I really am but . . ."

"I'm not done." He stood up and faced her again. "I haven't got to the end yet. It's unbelievable." He took a deep breath and continued. "I was going home one night. Driving. A couple of years ago. It was close to eleven o'clock. The coaches and the quarterbacks had been going over some movies and had started to work on next week's game plan. As I was driving I noticed that there was some kind of problem in the street ahead of me. I saw two police cars had stopped in the road. The red lights on one was flashing and a crowd was gathering. I rolled down my window as I slowed to a stop. Then it seemed like there were sirens coming from everywhere. Before I could move out I was hemmed in by police cars, policemen and people. So I parked and got out. I didn't know what had happened. Then I saw somebody down in the street next to a police car. As I got close I could see it was a policeman in uniform.

Barney paused and sat down on the hearth. He rested his elbows on his knees. His head was down and his voice was low. Mary strained to listen. She wanted to ask him to speak up but she could not.

"God, it was terrible. Almost all of his face was gone. I remember seeing one cop standing by his car crying like a baby. Two young high school kids holding hands and giggling ran up to take a look. They looked then threw up all over each other— still holding hands. I turned and walked away as an ambulance stopped in the middle of the street. Two men jumped out and ran over to the body. Then one went back and got a sheet and laid it over him. They both walked slowly back to the ambulance and drove away. I got to my car and tried to be sick too but couldn't. I had to sit there for the better part of an hour before I could drive away. And not just because of the crowd. I remember wondering who that poor cop was and if he had a family.

"The next morning I got up and started cooking my breakfast. I got the paper from out in the hall and sat down to eat. I always read the sports page first but I'd noticed the headlines, 'Police Officer Slain by Dope Addicts.' I started to read of what I'd seen the night before. Then I was really sick. It all came up then. That faceless mess in uniform I had seen lying in the street was Jake. Then I cried, too, just like that young cop. There hadn't been enough left for me to even recognize one of my best friends."

Barney stood up, walked from the fireplace and sat next to her. He kissed her lightly and held her close.

"I love you very much, Mary Beth, but please get out of that job. I've got a bad feeling about it, I've got some kind of premonition."

Mary felt herself falling asleep. She recalled Barney's foreboding that night as they had sat together by the fire. "I've got a premonition," he had said. Was it Barney's concern that was bothering her? No, it was something more than that. What nagged at her was trying to recall who had first expressed those words of concern, and when and where. It bothered her that for some unknown reason she was concerned about the source. She drifted off into a troubled sleep.

Part Six

The alarm on the electric clock woke Mary at 9:30 A.M. It was a blustery Friday morning and it was early for her considering that she usually slept a full eight hours. But she had lots to do.

Her one-bedroom apartment was always kept neat so making the bed and getting breakfast occupied her first half hour. At 10:00 she was wrapping the birthday gift, a beautiful pewter three-piece coffee service with a tray. She knew her mother would cry when she opened it, but would be happy because it would match the old pewter pieces she had received from Mary's father on their tenth wedding anniversary almost thirty years ago.

Mary knew also that her mother would mention her father, if only briefly. Together they would look at her father's picture and the memories would come flooding back for both of them. The photo was that of a smiling and handsome young man in a uniform almost identical to Mary's. It had been taken the day after her mother had proudly sewn on her father's sergeant's stripes and a month before he was shot to death. A similar photo, only larger, in a brass frame hung in the entryway of the police headquarters building. The inscription under her father's picture read, "Sergeant Michael A. Moore, killed in the line of duty by an armed felon." Mary had thought bitterly of that

210

inscription many times. The armed felon had become an ex-felon only twelve years after murdering her father. Then eight months after his release from prison he had been arrested again after murdering the proprietor of a small hardware store during a robbery.

Mary had warm memories of her father. She was only five years old when he had died but she could still remember him. She recalled his booming laugh and how he had always picked her and her sister up and hugged them when he awoke in the morning and went downstairs for breakfast. But most of all Mary remembered how he had looked in his uniform and the pride he'd had in wearing it. She remembered too, that one of her greatest disappointments as a child was when he had told her, after she had asked, "No, Honey Doll, little girls don't grow up to be policemen. Only boys do."

Mary backed her car out of the carport and began the drive across the city to her mother's house. Her sister would be there with her three-year-old, Michael Moore Ahern. They would have a good visit and discuss those things most important to them. She knew they would ask about Barney without asking what they really wanted to hear. Her mother and sister heartily approved of Barney, and she knew why. Maybe Barney would make her give up police work. She knew, given just one wish, both her mother and sister would wish her off the department. But this wish would never be mentioned aloud as Mary's work on the department, by mutual consent, was not discussed. At least not any more.

Mary remembered the day she finally told her mother she was going to become a policewoman. Knowing what her mother's feelings would be she had kept the well-guarded secret until the day before her graduation at the police academy. When she invited her mother to the graduation exercises and her mother had realized that her youngest daughter was to be one of the graduates, she broke down and wept.

It had turned out to be a horrible day. There was neither a quarrel, nor was there any bitterness. Mary tried not to feel guilty, but she realized she was the cause of her mother's sadness. Two weeks later her mother apologized. "Mary, please understand my feelings. You should know how I feel. It's because I love you so, dear. Of course I want you to do what you want with your life, but I have a premonition."

Mary turned up the street, three blocks from her mother's house. *There it was,* she thought. That's who had said it before. She remembered it was her mother who had mentioned "a premonition." But why did that bother her now? What premonition? Still, thought Mary, pulling to the curb in front of the yellow and white stucco home, it had been said even before that day—a long time before that. *What was its meaning and why can't I think of it? Oh well, forget it for now.*

It was 1:00 P.M. when she stepped out of her car and walked up the steps to her mother's house. Her sister and young Michael had already arrived.

As she had expected, her mother became tearful when she opened her gift. But she was happy too. "It's just beautiful, Mary," her mother said. "I'll put it on the hutch with the pewter your father gave me long ago." Mary saw her mother pause and pick up the picture of the young Sergeant Michael Moore. She touched the photo softly, then looking around she smiled and brushed some imaginary dust from the top of the frame. The photograph was replaced without comment.

The rest of the afternoon was spent touring her mother's beautifully manicured garden, and discussing young Michael Moore, her sister's husband—Dr. Jim, a promising young surgeon, and Barney.

At 4:15 PM Mary stood up and said, "Well, it's time I get to work." During the momentary silence Mary mentally kicked herself. *Why didn't I just say I have to leave?* She spoke briefly with her sister and told her to tell Dr. Jim, Hi. She mussed Michael's hair and he laughed and ran, wanting her to chase him.

"Bye Mom," then seeing the tears, she said, "Hey come on. I have Sunday off and if you're going to be home, I'll come over and we can watch Barney on TV. It's an away game and will be televised locally."

"Fine, Mary. I'll see you Sunday. I'll make a good lunch and we can eat while we're rooting for Barney. He's such a fine young man." She brushed her eyes. "Don't worry about me, dear. The tears are for your thoughtful gift. That's all."

But Mary wondered. Did the pewter cause the tears, or . . . ? As she drove west her thoughts centered on what was in store for her tonight. This Friday evening would be the real beginning of her career as a police officer.

Part Seven

Mary walked into the roll call room five minutes early. She placed her field briefcase on a chair and turned to walk toward the pin maps. Half of the night watch had already arrived and Mary could feel the men watching her. *Damn, damn,* she complained silently to herself. *They all know and I'm standing here*

213

starting to blush like a school girl on her first date. Then she saw John MacReadie in the second row and he flashed her a smile and gave her a thumbs up. She felt better.

Mary strolled nonchalantly, she hoped, to the north wall. It was covered with a series of 4 x 5 maps of the city. She moved to the well punctured map with its pins of plain red, and red with white crosses. She looked at her beat area in the northwest quadrant of the city. A good beat she thought. She knew it well. Small businesses, a large shopping mall and a nice residential district.

Then Lt. Stone arrived trailing teletypes and carrying his log book. He sat down behind the old oak table, then glanced up as a 45 second late straggler entered the room. Lt. Stone gave the man a sizzling look from beneath his bushy gray eyebrows. Nothing was said, but Mary, seated in the next to the last row, could see the lieutenant make a mark in his log book. She was glad she had been on time.

"Attention to the roll call."

The room became totally silent except for the lieutenant's voice and the response from the police officers.

"Mazzone."

"Here."
"Zebra 31."

"Remick."

"Ho."
"Zebra 28."

"Melendres."

"Here."
"Zebra 27."

"MacReadie."

"Sir."
"Zebra 24."

"Moore."

"Here, sir," Mary responded.
"Zebra 22."

The lieutenant continued with roll call. Mary picked up her pencil, circled the date on her hot sheet and across the top wrote 2 Zebra 22, then signed her name. A date to remember she thought to herself. I'm going to get this framed for posterity. I'll hang it in our den and someday Barney and I will laugh about it when we hand it down to our grandkids.

She thought of her mother and her eyes moistened. *Please Mom, try to understand my feelings too.* Then a bit of the Irish heritage sent her mind wandering. She thought of her father. He would have understood. Mary was convinced he would have. If he were still alive he might have been her watch commander, or even the Captain of this station. She looked at the big rectangular window on the west wall of the room. She smiled as she fantasized and created an image of her father, in full uniform, framed by the twilight seeping through the edges of the old venetian blinds. *I knew you would understand,* she nodded at her father.

As her father's image faded in the dusk she thought of Lieutenant Stone. He'd really taken it well. Mary couldn't recall even a little tremor in his voice as he read off her name and assigned her to a car by herself. She shook her head . . . the lieutenant . . .

roll call . . . damn. Suddenly, she realized the lieutenant had almost finished roll call and had been reading teletypes for several minutes. She cursed herself silently as she realized she'd missed some of it while daydreaming.

The lieutenant's voice droned on . . . "last seen driving a late model blue sedan, possibly a Ford. The first two digits in the license number are two four. The dicks are working on that trying to come up with the rest of it. So be on the watch for this pair. They were just hitting gas stations and small markets until three nights ago when they hit those two motels. Remember, armed and dangerous."

He paused and looked up. "Any questions?"

Mary thought, damn, I didn't get those descriptions, but I'm damned sure not going to ask now and let the lieutenant and all these guys know I wasn't paying attention. I'll get it later from MacReadie or read it off the teletypes.

The lieutenant's voice boomed out. "Okay, let's get to work. The day watch is waiting and wants to go home to mom and the kids."

At 1845 hours exactly, right on time, patrol officer Mary Beth Moore drove out of the police parking lot, alone in the big blue and white cruiser. With the greatest of confidence and pride she picked up the mike and reported, loud and clear, "2 Zebra 22, night watch, clear."

By 2000 hours, in a little more than an hour and a half, Mary had stopped and cited three motorists, two for speed and one for unsafe lane change. Mary thought it all very simple, and was slightly miffed when she noted that on two of her stops, her "brother" officers had cruised by, stopping momentarily to watch her. The second time she had waved the patrolmen off. She couldn't recall this attentive backup service when the men made their traffic stops.

She felt good after the third citation. Three was high for the average patrolman on a full eight hour tour of duty and she had three already with over six hours to go. She might even get a couple more before the night was done she thought. *My performance is going to be just fine, sergeant, I guarantee it.* Now to hunt up a couple of good FI's.

A few minutes past eight Mary received her first call. "See the woman, a family dispute, code 2." On arrival Mary talked to Mrs. Mallory at the scene. The dispute was between Mrs. Mallory and her seventeen-year-old fatherless son. Young Sal had punched his mother out, then had driven off in the car she needed to get to work. As Mary was taking the report from the distraught woman, who stubbornly refused to go to a hospital, Patrolman Ron Mazzone arrived.

"Need any help, Mary?"

"Nope, I put out a code 4, didn't you hear it?"

"I know, said Mazzone. "But I was passing by and I was just curious."

"I can handle it okay, Ron."

"Maybe I should stick around in case this punk comes back."

"If he does and I need you, I'll call. Okay?"

"Okay, Mary." Mazzone headed for the door. "No big deal."

Mary shook her head. Nice guy. All of them. But dammit, they're going to have to leave me alone on my calls.

She cleared at 2040 hours and almost immediately heard 2 Zebra 33 broadcast, "Code 4, suspect in custody at Johnson's Drug. Advise the alarm company their bell is still ringing."

She smacked her steering wheel with the palm of her hand. *Damn. While I'm taking that stupid report, Zebra 33 gets a burglar at the edge of my beat. I'll just have to go out and find one on my own to catch up.*

Five minutes later, Mary was racing to the east end of her beat to back up 2 Zebra 21 on a fight call in a bar parking lot. Approaching from the west on 17th Avenue and still a block away, she could see the revolving red lights of the police car and the crowd behind the bar. Mary hit the siren and coasted into the lot, scattering several onlookers. Officer Monte Williams had done a good job of beginning to get the situation under control. Both combatants, now ex-friends, were customers and had gone to the bar together to pick up a couple of girls. The problem began several drinks later when they both became interested in the same girl who enjoyed playing one against the other. The fight had started in the bar but had been quickly steered outside by the owner and his night bartender.

The two men, both battered and beaten, now turned their wrath on the police officers but were too exhausted to resist and were quickly separated and handcuffed. Both would be transported to the emergency ward of the city hospital and be patched up prior to being booked for assault and battery. It would be called a case of mutual combat.

Mary had learned the definition of mutual combat early in her career. Mutual combat was a crime usually committed on Friday night and then dismissed in the prosecutor's office on Monday morning. Apparently it mattered not to the "top" of the criminal justice hierarchy that thousands of dollars in time were wasted by hundreds of police officers, in all the fifty United States, every Friday and Saturday night, with the so-called mutual combat cases. The combatants, an almost always drunk husband and wife, boyfriend and girlfriend, or as in this case, two buddies, had to be taken into custody by the police to preclude further violence. Within 24 hours, however, a beaten wife would suddenly realize the guy that brought home the bacon was in jail instead of being at work. She would call frantically to advise the police she no longer desired to prosecute her husband. And so it goes with the boyfriend-girlfriend fight and the slugfest between the ex-friends. Nobody wants to prosecute so the prosecutor and the courts roll over and play dead. But the time consuming, money wasting, and not altogether undangerous drama, repeats itself weekend after weekend.

Mary wondered what would happen if a prosecutor would file such a case regardless of an "I don't want to prosecute" statement and the judge would ask the victim to testify. A probation sentence and a warning by the court would almost certainly preclude further weekend fisticuffs, and help the already overburdened police direct their attention to more appropriate endeavors. It seemed, she thought, guilt could be easily established beyond a reasonable doubt in such cases. But that sounded like a very simple solution. Maybe that was the problem, the solution was too simple for the high and the mighty of the criminal justice system to recognize.

At 2115 hours Mary was given a Code 7. She drove to Ringo's where she could get a barbecue sandwich and a coke brought to her in the car. No sense in taking a chance on missing anything. She listened to the radio as she ate.

At 2135 hours she cleared and ten minutes later pounced on a DUI attempting to drive east on westbound only Pepper Avenue. Ron Mazzone backed her up and this time Mary didn't growl at his presence. Ron agreed to impound the drunk's car and that would save her some time. She'd be able to get back on patrol at least 20 to 30 minutes sooner after she tested and booked her arrestee at the station.

Mary left the station driving north and hadn't gone two blocks before the small stumbling figure appeared in her headlights right in the middle of the road. She stopped her car and got out, then was surprised to see that the errant pedestrian was a little, gray-haired lady. Must be at least 90, Mary thought. She looks like what I've always imagined the little old lady from Pasadena would look like. Mary returned the walk-away to her residence, a nursing home for the elderly just three blocks from where Mary had found her.

At 2315 hours Mary was back on the prowl. This time with radio down low she parked under a big eucalyptus tree in a dark corner of the huge Southland Mall Shopping Center parking lot. Minutes before she'd cruised the fringe of the area, lights out and at a slow speed. She'd first seen the two men when they stopped their pickup next to two large sedans parked behind the Sears store. The stores were closed for customers, but Mary knew that on Friday nights the Sears office spaces were often used for Southland Mall executive conferences.

Now, under the big tree and in total darkness, Mary watched as the two men walked quickly to a big Continental. One of them raised a bar to the wind wing and in a matter of seconds, the left front door swung open. The clouters worked quickly as they carried their loot from the car to the truck.

Mary reached down with her left hand and quietly released the brake. The darkened police car rolled down the incline picking up speed as it approached the two busy thieves. Twenty feet from the pickup, Mary turned on all her lights: headlights, spot, and overhead reds. Startled, and trapped, the two young men threw down their loot and tools, put up their hands and meekly surrendered. Mary had them cuffed and secured in the back of her patrol car before she called and asked for a backup to assist in picking up the evidence and taking photos of the damaged Lincoln.

It was 20 minutes after midnight when Mary finished booking her two arrestees. That would look pretty good, she thought. My first DFAR will show two in the felony arrest box. But why just two? The best two hours, the last two of the watch, were coming up.

Back on the beat Mary thought of the chief's new policy on promotions. Two years on the job was the basic requirement in order to be eligible to take the sergeant's exam. She smiled to herself. Only eleven months left to show them all I can do it. Just imagine—Sergeant Mary Beth Moore. Why not?

"2 Zebra 22 see the man, a theft report." Mary rogered the call and drove west on Briarwood Avenue. She knew the address and she knew the owner, old Mr. Green. He had been there for many years in his small neighborhood grocery store. Mary had taken reports from him before and often stopped on the way home for some forgotten item. Mr. Green was very nice and Mary knew he was lonely too. He treated and appreciated the people who stopped by more as guests than as customers. And he stayed open late, but not as late as he used to.

About two months ago, he had been robbed and roughed up by two young stickup men when he was closing the store at 4:30 AM. Mary and John MacReadie had backed up on the call. She had helped him walk groggily to the ambulance. He was too proud to lie down on a stretcher. "No more late hours, Mary," he told her as he was helped into the rear of the ambulance. "When I come back I'm going to lock up at one o'clock. Tell all the policemen if they want to stop by to get here before then." Mary assured him that she would, and promised to see that the store was secured as the ambulance left for the hospital.

Mary pulled into the small parking lot a few minutes before 1:00. "Hi Mary, come on in, I'm getting ready to lock up. Where's your partner?" He peered through the partially opened glass front door at the police car.

"I'm on my own now Mr. Green, I don't have a partner any more."

"Jeez Mary," he shook his head. "Are you sure you'll be okay? There's some nasty people out there. I know from personal experience."

Mary sighed. "I'll be okay Mr. Green. I know what to do. I've had a year's training, a lot more than I needed. What happened in here anyway?"

"Two kids this time Mary."

"Shoplifters again?" She knew the local shoplifting set drove poor old Mr. Green up the wall.

"No, they tried to do that till thing. You know what I mean."

"Till tap?"

"Yeah, that's what you call it."

"How did they work it?"

"Well, the little one, must only have been ten years old, he asked me to help him get a box of crackers down from that top shelf." He pointed towards the wall in the rear of the store.

"I went over to help him. I was reaching up with my back turned when the other one tried to get into the cash register. But my new alarm went off and scared him. When I went for the bigger one, the little one ran out the front door, then the big one got away from me. I guess I'm just getting too darn old, Mary. That's my problem."

"You're doing just fine, Mr. Green, but you should be careful. Remember what happened the last time you tried to stop something like that in your store?"

"Well, I just didn't like to give up without a fight, Mary. I think we've got too much of this pantywaist stuff nowadays anyway. If more of us stood up against people like that maybe there wouldn't be so many crooks in the world."

Mary smiled. "You're right, Mr. Green, and I admire you for it, but be careful. You don't have the training we do." She took out her metal covered report book. "Ever see these kids before?"

"Yes, I think I know where the little guy lives. Just about four or five blocks from here. Don't know the address, but I can show you the house."

"Good, I'll follow you that way when we're done with this report. What about this new alarm you've been talking about, Mr. Green? How does it work?"

"Oh. I got two new alarms, Mary. Let me show you. Sergeant

Franklin, you know him?"

"Yes, he works Crime Prevention Division."

"Right, he's the one. He came over. He showed me how to hook up these alarms. They're both very simple."

He walked to his cash register and closed it. "I'll show you how this works. Whenever I leave the till I flip this little switch over to here. Now if I'm gone and anyone opens it," he pushed the No Sale button—the tray slid back and a buzzer sounded. "How about that?" He laughed as Mary nodded approvingly.

"Now, here is the other one. Sergeant Murphy, he's the one that worked on the robbery, he thought this one up and Sergeant Franklin helped me install it."

Mr. Green walked to his front door and pointed across the street. "See over there, the Nightlamp Motel?"

Mary walked to the front door, looked out the window and nodded.

"Well," continued the store owner, "We have rigged up a 'help your neighbor' alarm system. That's what Sergeant Franklin calls it. He says it's part of the Neighborhood Watch Program. You know about that, I suppose?"

Mary smiled. "I know about that. I wish more people would find out about it."

"We have wires running through that culvert from my place to the motel. That's the culvert right over there."

They both looked as Mr. Green pointed at the grate covered hole under the street. It ran from the corner of the grocery store lot to where the sign stood in front of the large U-shaped motel. As they watched a sedan stopped under the covered port of the motel entrance. Two people got out of the car and walked casually into the motel office.

"Now," Mr. Green continued, "if I get robbed or they get robbed, we just throw this little switch here."

Mr. Green leaned over and pointed to a small switch under the cash register. "Here's what happens. Say the Sloanes over at the motel are getting held up. Mr. or Mrs. Sloane would push a switch, just like this one. Over here at my place this little light blinks and beeps at me. Then I call for you, Mary, simple as that."

"I hope you don't accidentally hit the switch and we get called when nothing is wrong. We run pretty hot on a robbery in progress call, Mr. Green."

"Oh we won't let that happen. I forgot to tell you. If that light goes on and the beeps starts, I telephone the motel. If there is no answer, I call you. If the Sloanes answer their phone and tell me the code, if they tell me, 'Sorry you have the wrong number, this is not McDonald's drugstore,' then I know there's bad trouble and I call the police. If they hit the switch accidentally, then of course they will tell me and I don't call. Pretty nifty, huh?"

"That's really great, Mr. Green. I wish more business people would do that." Mary opened her report book. "Now let's get on this report so I can get back to work and you can go home." Mary looked at her watch and filled in the date and the time report taken boxes.

'Okay, Mr. Green, what time did those kids come into your

store?" She looked up as the suddenly startled store owner stepped back and away from his cash register. A little red light was blinking rapidly and a series of electronic beeps kept perfect time with the small flashing bulb.

"I hope that's just a coincidence." He glanced apprehensively at Mary.

"Call them up. That's what you're supposed to do isn't it?"

"Yeah, yeah, it's just that I've never done this before and it makes me nervous."

Mr. Green ran his index finger down a list of numbers on a sheet of paper on his counter, stopped at one, picked up the phone and dialed. Finally, he spoke into the mouthpiece, "This is Mr. Green." Mary watched as his face drained of color. Then he hung up. "My God, Mary, that was Mr. Sloane. He told me, I'm sorry you have the wrong number. This is not McDonald's drugstore. Then he hung up on me. They're being robbed at the motel."

Mary's heart began pounding. A robbery in progress. What a break. I'm right in position to get me a couple of stickup men. She turned to Mr. Green and spoke quickly. "Call our emergency number. Tell them of the robbery. Be sure and tell them I'm already at the scene. I'm going over on foot. I'll leave my car out front so I won't scare them off."

"Okay, Mary, I'll call. Please be careful. Wait for the men, remember you're just a . . ."

Mary walked out of the door, her face burning crimson. "Jesus," she mumbled, "now I have to convince the citizens too. Well now's the time." As she reached the curb she looked back over

226

her shoulder and saw Mr. Green speaking into the phone.

Part Eight

Mary drew her gun and walked quickly across the street toward the edge of the wall leading to the motel office. She glanced at the automobile in the carport. As she got closer she could see that it was a blue Ford, license number 247 Henry Ocean. *That's it. That's the car the robbery suspects are working in.* Then thinking back, she cursed herself momentarily. She had missed the suspects' descriptions when the lieutenant had read them off, at roll call. That's what she got for daydreaming about her new-found glory, instead of paying attention. Too late now, she thought, but in a minute or so it won't matter. I'll be able to get their exact descriptions when I bust the both of them.

Slowly she made her way to the door of the well-lighted office, noting that it was slightly ajar. Now she could see Mr. and Mrs. Sloane standing behind the counter. Mr. Sloane had one arm around his wife's shoulder and the other at an awkward half-mast position. They both looked terrified. Then Mary saw one of the holdup men. He had moved forward and stood close to the Sloanes, his back to the door and Mary. Where was the other guy she wondered? Probably looting the Sloane's living quarters.

Far off in the distance a low whine began to rise and fall. A siren. Mary was sure that would be Mac. His beat boundary was next to hers, just two miles away. *Good old Mac,* she thought, *he'll be here first and knowing him, he'll be proud of me for grabbing these two bandits.* She tightened her grip on the revolver, stepped quietly up to the doorway, and stopped. She pushed open the door slightly and pointed the gun at the midpoint of the man's back. Her voice was steady and clear. "Police officer, freeze. Drop the gun and turn around slow, real slow, both hands up and in sight."

"Don't shoot, don't shoot, officer." The man had stiffened at the voice behind him. A large automatic fell on the carpeted floor. He turned around, raised his hands and looked at Mary. "Oh shit. Don't shoot lady. Take it easy now. Don't pull that trigger, I'll behave."

Mary stepped through the door. The Sloanes hadn't moved a muscle.

"Where's your partner?"

"What partner?"

"Dammit, I know there's another guy with you. Where'd he go, Mr. Sloane?"

The motel manager looked like he wanted to answer, but the bandit spoke instead. "No way, Ma'am." He shrugged his shoulders and started to lower his hands. "Nobody here but me. All you got is just me."

"Get those hands up. I saw both of you guys come in this place."

"Yes Ma'am, anything you say. I just never seen a lady cop before, that's all."

Mary started to query the two victims again when a young girl suddenly appeared in the doorway leading to the Sloanes' apartment. Startled, she stopped quickly. She looked at the robber, then at Mary.

Mary spoke first. "Don't worry, Miss. There has been a robbery. Come into the room and get out of the way. One of the suspects could still be close by, but help is on the way." The siren was very close now, and could easily be heard by the four people in the room.

Mary thought her prisoner was tensing up to jump her and she stepped back and faced him as the young woman moved behind her. Then, simultaneously it seemed, Mary heard two voices, a scream, then two shots.

Mr. Sloane yelled, "Look out." But his warning was partially drowned out by Mrs. Sloane's piercing scream. The robber, hands still held high, clenched his fists and shouted, "Shoot, for Christ's sake do it quick, they're almost here."

Then the two shots. Mary felt two heavy thumps on her back that made her stagger forward. The first hurt for only an instant, a second or two, then there was no pain. Mary turned as she began to fall. She looked back and saw the girl holding a snub-nosed revolver in her hand. *My God,* thought Mary, *a man and woman stickup team, and I let that woman shoot me in the back.*

She fell on her side and watched the two suspects as they ran through the door toward their car. She could hear Mr. Sloane on the phone telling somebody a police officer had been shot. Then, best of all, she heard the shredding of tires on asphalt and a siren so loud it sounded like the police car was coming through the front door. Good old Mac, he was here. The robbers would not get away now

It bothered her that she could not move. Maybe some kind of shock, she thought. There was no pain at all. She tried to call out to MacReadie to warn him that the robbers were armed and that it was a man and woman bandit team. Oh hell, she thought, he'd already know that. He'd listened to the lieutenant. She was the only one that had goofed at roll call and had missed the descriptions.

Suddenly she heard several shots; small arms fire. Then the night was split by several thunderous explosions that rattled the windows of the motel office. Two, then three, booming blasts. *Shotguns,* Mary thought. It sounds like the guys got here in time all right. The robbers wouldn't stand a chance against that double ought buck.

Mary looked down to make sure she was still lying on the carpet. For a moment it felt as though she were starting to float away. She tried to move her hand up to brush some hair out of her eyes but the hand remained motionless at her side. Nothing would move. The scream of sirens seemed to be filling the early morning air. They were coming from every direction and were converging on the motel. She looked up as MacReadie burst into the room, shotgun at ready. He stopped, looked at Mary, then knelt beside her. "Mary! Where are you hit, Mary?" Then he drew his hand quickly away from her back. "Oh Jesus Christ Almighty." He jumped up and stepped to the door. "Ron," he yelled into the night, "Tell that ambulance to get going. Floor it. Mary's down. She's been hit, real bad I think."

Mary tried as best she could to tell Mac it wasn't that bad. There was no pain, she was just going to be a little numb for a while. But she couldn't say the words. She could see okay, and hear too, but several times in the last few minutes she noticed that funny floating sensation.

She watched as several officers appeared at the door but Mac wouldn't let them in. She closed her eyes. Then, opening her eyes she saw Sergeant Matthews come in. That's funny, Mary

230

thought. He looks like he's walking in slow motion.

She wanted very much to tell her sergeant she was sorry, but she couldn't talk. He knelt down and picked up her hand. She saw him squeeze it, but for some strange reason she couldn't feel his hand on hers. She looked up into his face. He smiled, or tried to, Mary thought. She noticed his face was almost chalk white. Then Sergeant Matthews got up and walked to the door. He kicked it viciously as he stepped outside. Suddenly Mary heard him shout into the night, "Son of bitch," he screamed. "You dirty rotten scum. You shot one of my police officers you bastards, and I'm glad you're dead." Then he sat down on the stairs and held his head in his hands.

Mary started to float again and for the first time her vision was blurred. She smiled though as she thought of the sergeant's words. He had referred to her as a police officer—finally. But she hoped the chief had not been outside to hear the sergeant's swearing.

Her vision cleared a little. She looked at Sergeant Matthews outside on the steps and wondered why he was shaking. It really wasn't that cold a night.

Now another siren wailed to a stop outside the motel office. Mary opened her eyes, they were becoming heavy and it bothered her. She knew she shouldn't be so sleepy this early. She saw the two men in firemen's uniforms enter the room as Mac stepped aside for them. She had seen them before, the paramedics from Station 6. The youngest looked like one of the actors on Emergency. He was the one that was always smiling. She knew they were touching her and looking at her back. She heard the scissors cutting into her jacket and shirt but couldn't feel anything. She glanced up and looked at the young fireman's face, she tried to smile but couldn't, but he wasn't smiling either.

Her vision wasn't improving, Mary realized. Things blurred more easily now. She closed her eyes and tried to relax. Then she thought she heard Barney's voice and once she thought she saw him standing next to MacReadie. But Barney couldn't be here, he was in New York. When she opened her eyes again he was gone. Her eyes closed slowly again.

When she opened her eyes again she saw the stars. There was the North Star. She could see it sparkling off the open end of the Big Dipper. She was in camp. Lone Pine summer camp. The camp leader was telling her that if she remembered how to find the North Star she would never get lost. She had always remembered that. Then Mary realized she was not at Lone Pine. She was on a stretcher in the motel parking lot. She saw Mr. Greene and noticed that Ron Mazzone had his arm around him holding him up. Poor old man Mary thought, he shouldn't be out this late. He must be very tired.

She saw that the parking lot was full of squad cars and policemen. They were all standing very still watching her. For some reason they had become very silent. Then she was being lifted into the back of an ambulance. Out of the corner of her eye she saw two white sheets on the asphalt next to the blue Ford. She could see the form of a body under each sheet. She saw a police car parked next to the blue Ford. The cruiser's windshield was shattered and punctured by at least four bullet holes. Mac-Readie, still at her side, seemed to sense her silent pleading question. He turned to her, leaned down and spoke in her ear. "It's O.K. Mary. It's none of us. It's both of them."

As the door slammed shut and the ambulance sped towards the hospital Mary thought it was very strange, I'm right inside this thing, but the siren seems so far away.

She opened her eyes slowly then tried to shake her head. She could tell she was still in the ambulance. She saw MacReadie, but now her sister and Barney were sitting next to the officer. He didn't seem to know they were both there. They both held out their hands towards her and she could read their lips. Barney was saying it again, "Please Mary, please, I've got a premonition." She looked at her sister, and she said very plainly, "Mary, we were very small when she said it. Remember? We were at the funeral."

Mary closed her eyes. They were trying to tell her about that premonition and a funeral. But what funeral? She opened her eyes again but Barney and her sister were gone.

The doors of the ambulance suddenly swung open. She looked up and saw three doctors and several nurses at her side as she was wheeled into the hospital. It must not be a busy night, Mary thought. She'd been at this hospital many times before and had never noticed doctors and nurses meeting the ambulances as they arrived.

She smiled a bit as she was wheeled down the hall and into a big brightly lit room. Everybody was moving in slow motion. She knew they weren't really, but it looked that way.

She closed her eyes and waited. A voice spoke very softly but clearly in the background. "No, I don't think so. One has severed the spine completely. That's the reason there is no pain. Both slugs have caused massive internal damage and hemorrhage. I'm sorry. Tell them to hurry with her as fast as they can. There's not much time left and there's nothing we can do. We'll start surgery in less than a minute now, of course, but I'm afraid it's too late." Then the click of a phone being reseated.

Mary frowned. That didn't make much sense to her. I wish they'd get me out of this emergency room and get me up to another room so I can be by myself.

Then she felt the presence of the person standing next to her. She could not feel the hand, but looking down she could see the huge hand covering her much smaller one. She looked up. It was very hard to focus her eyes now. Then she could see it was Lieutenant Stone. *Now that isn't right,* she thought. *He is supposed to be at the station.* She distinctly remembered having read the department manual, and it was very plain. The watch commander could only leave the station in emergencies of great priority. That was sure to be a question on the next sergeant's exam.

Tears streamed down Lieutenant Stone's face. She squinted her eyes. Blurred vision again? But no, they were tears and it was Lieutenant Stone. She tried again to talk but couldn't. She wanted desperately to tell the lieutenant she was sorry for not listening at roll call and missing those descriptions.

Lieutenant Stone's face seemed to fade away. She closed her eyes, then opened them again. Now the Chief was standing next to Lieutenant Stone. God, thought Mary, how he's aged since he met with us a couple of weeks ago. He looks like he's twenty years older. Then the Chief and Lieutenant Stone faded away.

She was lifted, she knew. The doctors and nurses were around her again. Now they were doing something with her back. Her eyes closed again.

The voice seemed to come from far away. Then it was said again, "I've got a premonition," but this time a woman's voice, and from deep in the past. She recognized the voice. It was her mother's. Then she remembered. It had been her mother who had said it first after all.

Mary looked around her. They were all standing on a hillside.

234

There were many people, most of them uniformed police officers. Even though the bright sunny day had suddenly become overcast all the policemen were wearing their sunglasses. A chilling wind caused the people assembled to draw up their collars and button up their coats. Mary saw her sister. Her sister was seven, two years older than Mary. Then a big black car stopped by the roadside and she saw her young mother sag against the arms of Mary's two uncles. The policemen then all stood at attention and put their hands up to their hats as the big flower-covered casket was carried across the grassy slope.

Mary was old enough to know that her father had been killed and that he was under all those flowers. Then Mary sat down next to her mother and sister under a tent. All the people gathered around them and a man talked about her father. Then a big man in a uniform gave a folded American flag to her mother. Mary thought her mother was in some kind of a trance. After a while almost all the people had gone away. Only Mary, her sister, her uncles and her mother remained. Then her mother stood up and slowly walked alone to the coffin. She placed the folded flag on top of the flowers, then knelt and put her hands on the casket. She bowed her head and Mary heard her say, "Oh dearest Michael, I wanted to tell you but I could not get up the courage for fear you would worry. I just knew dear Michael, I had a premonition . . ."

Now Mary thought, I know at last.

It seemed to her that even when she could hold her eyes open that the light in the hospital room was getting darker. Then she heard, very faintly, a door open in the corner of the room. A moment later, next to her, a voice cried out, "Oh my dear God, my poor baby." It was her mother's voice again. But she was not dreaming of her father's funeral now. She knew her mother was in the room . . . now standing next to her . . . She heard her cry out again . . . "Oh, my poor baby, I just knew . . . I had a pre-monition."

Mary tried to open her eyes . . . tried to call out to her mother . . . but she could not . . . she felt herself floating away again . . . but this time she could not stop.

It was very dark now . . . then it was very quiet.

beware of the "typical... average..."

12

beware of the "typical . . . average . . ."   12

Statistics, depending on source, method of collection and presentation, can either be accurate or deviously misleading and frustrating. The FBI is the primary statistical gathering agency that we depend upon for accuracy regarding the number of police officers killed and assaulted. Much of the material in this chapter comes from four FBI publications:

Crime in the United States—1973, and, *Law Enforcement Officers Killed Summary, 1972, 1973* and *1974.*

During the ten year period 1965 through 1974, 940 law enforcement officers were feloniously slain in the United States and Puerto Rico. A very basic statistic, the average, is readily apparent. On the average, 94 police officers have been murdered every year in the past ten years. But 64 per cent of those 940 were killed in the last five-year reporting period, which makes the "average" for the last three years 126 officers killed each year.

A statistical review reveals the following:

The deadly weapon: In the last five year reporting period, 1970-1974, 583 police officers have been murdered by guns in the *hands* of their killers. But 28 officers were killed by other weapons, too.

Conclusion: Guns are the most deadly, but not always.

When did the officers die? In 1972, the greatest percentage of officers were killed between 10:00 PM and 11:00 PM, but in 1973 the greatest percentage of officers were killed between 1:00 AM and 2:00 AM and between 2:00 PM and 3:00 PM. In 1974, 1:00 AM to 2:00 AM was the deadly hour.

Conclusion: There are no "safe hours." Police officers have been killed during *every* hour of the day and night.

Is there a "most dangerous day?" During 1972, most policemen were killed on Wednesday and Saturday (20 each day). In 1973, most died on Sunday (24). But in 1968, more officers were killed on Monday and Tuesday (13 each day), and in 1970 and 1971, Friday was "high point" day (19, then 28). Thursday has never been "high" but between 1968 and 1974, 107 officers have been killed on that particular day of the week.

Conclusion: It can happen on any day.

Which month? Most officers have died in January since 1968 (77). Since 1968, along with January, the months of February, April, May, June, July and December have also been high months for the year. March is the low month, but still 46 officers have died in March through the 1968-1974 reporting period.

242

Conclusion: Don't relax if you make it through January.

How about police officers killed related to population groups? In 1973, 46 of the 134 police officers murdered were killed in cities of over 250,000. But over 50 percent of all officers killed died in rural and suburban counties and cities with populations of less than 25,000.

Conclusion: With the increase in suburban crime the odds are there will be more police officer funerals in the suburbs.

What type of activity was the officer engaged in when he lost his life?

Prisoner transport: in the four years 1971 through 1974, 21 police officers lost their lives.

Mentally deranged persons have accounted for 12 police officer deaths in the three year period, 1971 through 1973.

During *civil disorders,* in 1971, 1972 and 1973, three officers died.

In the four year reporting period, 1971-1974, 36 police officers were killed *investigating suspicious circumstances* or *persons.*

Surprisingly, the *ambush slaying* of police officers dropped from 20 in 1971, to 14 in 1972, to zero in 1973. But seven officers died in unprovoked ambush murders in 1974.

Felonious criminal attack during *traffic pursuits* and *traffic stops* between 1971 and 1974 cost the lives of 70 police officers.

Ninety-four policemen were killed in the four year period, 1971-1974, *attempting arrests* other than for *burglary* and

243

robbery.

Responding to *disturbance calls,* primarily family disturbance calls (known to all police officers as a situation with a high potential for violence) led to the deaths of 85 law enforcement officers during the 1971-1974 reporting period.

Finally, and highest as always, *responding* to *burglary* and *robbery in progress* calls. Of the 134 police officers killed while involved in this type activity, 102 were killed while responding to robberies in progress or pursuing robbery suspects.

It is important to note that not all police killers are adult males. Women kill police officers. The percentage is not high, but in 1973 four percent of the 134 officers who died were killed by females. In 1972 one woman killed two police officers in a gun battle after committing an armed robbery. Do juveniles and older people kill policemen? In 1972, the youngest police killer was 13, the oldest 73. In 1973 the situation improved (?). The youngest was 15, the oldest only 67.

All the statistics related above are factual and they are significant. There is no "typical" or "average" situation. Certainly more police officers are murdered responding to felony in progress calls. But some officers are killed responding to seemingly non-violent and routine calls. I believe that the great majority of police officers know better than to rely on the supposed "typically" described killer who will attack at the "most likely" time of day or night after having a few beers at the local pub. And there is no "average" description of the police killer. When the murderers range in age from 13 to 73, and a female can kill two police officers in a single incident, the police can't afford to watch for the profile of the "average" killer.

Police officers have been killed every hour of every day, on each

244

of the seven days of the week, during every one of the twelve months of the year. It can happen at any time.

It can also happen in any place. Big city, small city, suburbs, rural, open highways, and cluttered ghetto alley. On April 5, 1970, the California Highway Patrol lost four fine young officers in less than five minutes time during a blazing gun fight with two armed men in a rural area a good many miles north of the Los Angeles megalopolis.

Two-man cars versus one-man cars? Are police officers safer working together or working alone? The statistics seem to indicate the controversy has been solved at last, or has it? In two years, 1972 and 1973, 71 policemen were killed riding alone versus 52 killed while riding with a partner. But the statistics may be deceptive. How many police officers ride alone throughout the country versus how many ride with a partner? Forget the one-man, two-man car controversy. Stay alert with or without a partner.

In 1974, of the 123 incidents (132 deaths) resulting in police officer murders, 57 of the officers killed were with one or more policemen at the time of their deaths. In 8 of the 123 incidents, 2 or more officers were killed at the same time. In the three year period, 1972-1974, 6 officers were killed while on foot patrol, 27 detectives working alone were killed and 39 policemen were killed in "off-duty" incidents.

Finally, what were the murderers doing at the time they became killers of police officers? Drunk? Yes, many were. But not all.

Many were committing an armed robbery or a burglary, or as we all know, killed an officer during a family quarrel. But what about the others? A review of the record reveals that police officers were killed by people who were:

Being booked,
Poaching for bears,
Poaching for deer,
Stripping a car,
DUI,
Traffic violators,
Cashing bad checks,
In custody enroute to jail,
Trespassing on private property,
Shoplifting,
Hitch-hiking,
Passenger in a DUI car,
Double parked,
Quarreling in the street,
Fighting in a bar,
Changing license plates,
Cattle rustling,
In jail as a trustee,
Involved in a business dispute,
Attempting suicide,
Driving a mechanically defective vehicle,
Selling narcotics,
Selling "moonshine,"
Stealing from a railroad car,
Being persuaded (and appeared to be ready) to surrender,
Walking up to a police officer writing a report in a patrol car,
Being administered an alcoholic content examination,
Being served with a misdemeanor warrant,
Being pursued in a vehicle chase,
Involved in an extortion,
Involved in an arson,
Committing a vandalism,
Committing a petty theft,
Running a police highway blockade,
Standing by a stalled vehicle,

Sitting at a bus stop.

There is no way to describe a typical killer or predict what time of day he, or she, will strike. Police officers can be killed at any time, in any place, and either on-duty or off-duty, by almost any kind of person who might be involved in the most obviously dangerous and explosive circumstance, or in the most innocent appearing situation.

post-mortem 13

post-mortem 13

The several cases which make up this book have described incidents in which police officers were killed or seriously injured in the line of duty by felonious criminal action. In each case the officer involved committed one or more of the identified deadly errors.

The cases involving Sergeant Clint Ramsey, Officers Bob Whitehead, Ted Blackman, Ken Dewey, Carl, David and the others who died, are not make-believe examples to prove a point. To be sure the names are fictitious but the "why" of how they died is not fictitious, it is a fact. Only the ending of the last story, "A Premonition" is a fiction. But I have a premonition regarding how much longer it will remain fiction.

This chapter, other than a summary and review—or post-mortem, provides recommendations and guidelines to assist any law enforcement agency, or any police officer, in establishing policy, procedures, and rules relevant to police officer survival.

Again, as was emphasized in one of the cases presented, the recommendations and guidelines are presented as suggestions only. Each department should establish its own policy, procedures and rules relating to the protection and survival of its police officers.

Most departments will find that the recommendations suggested are acceptable for use without alteration. Understandably, policy, procedures and rules will not necessarily be identical in each case for every department, any more than policy, procedures and rules can be written to cover every contingency that might arise in the day-to-day operations of a law enforcement agency.

A general policy guideline for the follow-up of cases related to officer-involved shootings, or in any case where a police officer is killed in the line of duty, is suggested below:

In every instance of an officer-involved shooting, and when any person involved is either injured or killed as a result of the shooting, or a police officer is killed during a felonious criminal assault, a team of specially trained detectives shall be notified immediately and shall respond to the scene to conduct the investigation.

The special team shall be deployed so that at least two detectives and one supervisor are available to respond at any time.

The team shall accurately report all facts of every case (regardless of the consequences).

All witnesses are to be interviewed.

Photographic reconstruction of the incident shall be accomplished at the scene, if possible.

The investigator's report is to be approved by the division captain, and copies shall be forwarded to the Chief of Police and to each member of the department command staff for review.

In coordination with Training Division the special team of investigators shall make lecture presentations to academy classes, both recruit and in-service, and to division roll calls throughout the city, frankly discussing the facts and details of the incident, particularly those deemed significant in the police officer street survival lecture series.

Additionally a board composed of at least three to five members of the command staff of the department shall review the investigative report and conduct an administrative hearing. They shall interview any or all persons involved in order to make recommendations to the Chief of Police. The recommendations may include:

a). a request for further investigation,
b). disciplinary action, or,
c). commendatory action.

Earlier, the causes of police officers killed unnecessarily were identified as the "ten deadly errors:"

1. Failure to maintain weapon, vehicle, and equipment proficiency and care.
2. Improper search and use of handcuffs.
3. Sleeping on duty.
4. Relaxing too soon.
5. Missing the danger signs.
6. Taking a bad position.
7. Failure to watch their hands.
8. Tombstone courage.

9. Preoccupation.
10. Apathy.

Policy, procedures and rules can be written relating to the first three: failure to maintain weapon proficiency and care of equipment; improper search and use of handcuffs; and sleeping on duty.

All police officers should be provided with an excellent service weapon, either a revolver or automatic, and ammunition.

Considerable study has been done on the kind of weapon an officer should use. Each department should carefully evaluate the type of weapon it chooses prior to making any final decision. The capability of the automatic to fire more rounds of ammunition before reloading should be carefully weighed against the revolver, which will fire all rounds of ammunition, though fewer in number, without jamming. The extra three rounds are of no help to the officer in a fire fight if his gun jams on the second shot.

Department policy should require all officers to have the same kind of gun and ammunition. Ideally, all police officers should be made to qualify on an approved firearms range at least once a month, certainly not less than once every two months.

Proper department inspection procedures by supervisory personnel should negate the possibility of any officer carrying anything other than a clean and serviceable weapon.

Police officers should not only be trained in how to shoot, they should be well trained in when and when not to shoot. Police officers should not be restricted to a rule that would prevent them from drawing their weapon unless they know they will have to fire. Police officers should be allowed to draw their weapons at any time they truly believe they are about to become involved in a situation that has a great potential for violence, or in which they might have to fire their weapons.

Department policy should require proper care and use of police vehicles. Misuse should be considered unacceptable and such conduct should be subject to appropriate disciplinary action. It is the duty of police officers to pursue criminals and traffic violators. Rules such as those that require a police officer to not pursue above a predetermined speed, are not only impractical but an invitation to a small but dangerous group of drivers who would then exceed that limit, knowing they would most probably not be pursued and apprehended.

During high-speed pursuits, rules of good judgment and common sense should prevail. There will be times when an officer, on his own initiative or on the order of a superior, should cease and desist from further pursuit. These few instances of aborted pursuit should not be viewed as faint-hearted or timorous conduct by the officer. Police officers and citizens have died unnecessarily in high-speed pursuits of subjects wanted for speed violation only, or even for auto theft. I fail to see a balance in favor of society when a speeder or an auto thief escapes, or is later captured, while the pursuing officer or an innocent citizen might die. I firmly believe a reasonable and prudent attempt must be made to apprehend in every case.

It is the responsibility of the police chief executive of the law enforcement agency to determine by testing, or receipt of information from those agencies that have the capability to conduct such tests, the safest and most economical police package vehicle for his officers to drive. It is the responsibility of the "city fathers" to provide the equipment requested, upon proper justification by the Chief. This is one instance where low bid and favoritism to local "hometown" dealers should be disregarded. Only if the tested and acceptable police package desired can be delivered should the local car dealer insignia be seen on the rear trunk door of the police car on patrol.

Composing policy concerning search, use of handcuffs, and sleeping on duty is a relatively simple management chore. Most departments will have (I hope) a policy regarding sleeping on duty—but how many aggressively enforce the policy? One tragic incident was cited in this case book. Usually, sleeping on duty results in missed calls for service, not in the death of a police officer. But what if the missed call for service results in the unnecessary death of a citizen? Sleeping on duty is a management problem. It's really up to you, Chief!

Many departments do not have procedures or rules relating to search and use of handcuffs. Policy should require that every person taken into custody be searched by the officer taking custody of the subject. A good and safe rule will also require a search to be made any time the responsibility of custody changes from one officer to another.

An interesting case regarding search occurred in California a few years ago. The subject was apparently hitchhiking when he was seen by two police officers in a patrol car. The officers volunteered to drive the subject to his stated destination, but frisked him prior to letting him enter the police car. Contraband (narcotics) was found during the search. The court held that the officers were justified in making a pat down search even in this non-arrest type situation to insure their safety prior to placing the man in the police car.*

*People versus Superior Court in and for the County of Marin, 110 Cal Reporter 875, California Appellate, 1973.

The following is quoted from a memo of one department relating to use of handcuffs. Incidents which justify the use of handcuffs are included following the policy:

The handcuffs shall be attached with the subjects' hands behind their backs. The cuffs shall be looped through, or attached to the subjects' belts, or used in such a manner to preclude the subject bringing the cuffs to a position in front.

A person arrested for a felony shall be handcuffed.

A person arrested for a misdemeanor may at the officer's discretion be handcuffed. It is encouraged that persons arrested for intoxication or driving under the influence of narcotics or alcohol be handcuffed.

A juvenile should not be handcuffed, *except* juveniles in custody for violent crimes, juveniles who physically resist arrest, or if in the opinion of the officer, the juvenile may attempt escape, or is a danger to himself or others.

The following incidents have been documented in the past year and illustrate the necessity of this policy regarding the securing of persons arrested for alcohol related cases:

Situation No. 1

A police officer arrested a white male at a local tavern for drunkenness and resisting arrest. The subject was an administrative official for the state. After the arrest, the subject identified himself, calmed down, and stated that he would not cause any more trouble. The handcuffs were removed. After approximately three minutes, the man again became violent and had to be subdued and re-handcuffed by five police officers.

Situation No. 2

Two officers arrested a woman for being drunk in public. Since there were two officers and the woman was just drunk, they did not handcuff her. Enroute to jail, she became violent and during the ensuing fight caused the driver of the police car to strike a parked car, injuring both officers and allowing her to temporarily escape.

Situation No. 3

A police officer in another suburban city stopped a vehicle sus pecting a drunk driver. The officer determined the driver was under the influence of alcohol and he was arrested. The arrestee observed the officer reaching for his handcuffs and pleaded with the officer not to handcuff him. As the officer was in the process of returning the handcuffs to their case, the arrestee pulled a small handgun from his waistband and shot the officer. The officer later said he decided not to handcuff the arrestee because the man had identified himself as a county employee. The man had never been arrested, and he did not appear to be a violent type. The arrestee could offer no explanation for shooting the officer.

Situation No. 4

Two police officers arrested a woman for criminal mischief. The officers did not handcuff her and placed her in the rear of the patrol car. She became violent and damaged the rear window of the patrol car by kicking it or striking it with her hands. The woman was five foot five and weighed 120 pounds. She had been drinking but not enough to be charged with public intoxication.

Situation No. 5

An officer arrested a drunk driver who had been involved in a minor traffic accident. The driver complained of an injured ankle and was taken to the county hospital. At the hospital he appealed to the officer to take the handcuffs off as they were embarrassing him. The officer removed the handcuffs and they were immediately grabbed from his hands by the arrestee who then struck the officer in the face with the handcuffs. The arrestee was subdued with the assistance of the hospital staff. The officer lost several teeth and sustained severe cuts on his face and head.

Summary

Experienced police officers, everywhere, will always handcuff:

1) Felons,

2) Persons who are intoxicated,

3) Persons who have been involved in an altercation,

4) When transporting any arrestee.

The fourth through seventh of the deadly errors, relaxing too soon, missing the danger signs, taking a bad position, and failure to "watch their hands," are factors more related to training than set in policy, procedures and rules.

Training by knowledgeable and experienced professionals, initially during basic training and then followed by on-going departmental roll call and in-service training, should provide information adequate enough to alert officers to the dangers of being unaware of these deadly errors. This type training should emphasize and be based on the following series of basic admonitions.

There are circumstances (several rather obvious) that warrant exceptional alertness by police officers rather than inactive non-vigilance. For example:

1) All contacts made under circumstances that require an inquiry with an unknown subject, particularly in a high risk crime area;

2) All instances of prisoner transportation from time of accepting custody until the subject is in complete control and custody of another police officer;

3) All traffic stops, at least until the officer is satisfied that the potential danger does not exist or has been neutralized;

4) All domestic disputes;

5) All unknown trouble calls;

6) All calls indicating that physical violence or a verbal altercation is in progress; and,

7) All felony in progress calls, or the reported possibility of a felony in progress.

The admonition to "watch their hands" is easily emphasized by a reminder that the weapons, primarily guns, used to murder police officers were held in no other place but the murderer's hands.

Tombstone courage, the eighth of the deadly errors, is the one that hurts the most. In every instance, courage was involved. And it is very difficult to do anything but extol the heroics of the officer as he is being buried. Criticism, even constructive criticism, directed towards the deceased officer following his being killed in action is not looked upon favorably, and would undoubtedly be taken as a form of heresy toward police traditionalism regarding our fallen heroes.

I have, during my lectures, stated that in my opinion police officers become heroes the day they are sworn in and receive their badges. That they have accepted the position is proof enough. It is neither practical nor necessary to be lowered into the ground in a plush pine box in order to establish a reputation as a courageous police officer. The popular TV police lieutenant said it all one night, as I watched him console a detective who had just seen his courageous partner shot to death. "Dead is not guts," said the lieutenant, "dead is dumb."

The ninth and tenth in the list of deadly errors, preoccupation and apathy, are factors primarily related to attitude. Obviously a poor or apathetic attitude stems from a lack of policy, poor procedures, unenforced rules and little or no training.

Police officers are people. They react like people. Recognition of this fact, I'm sure, would surprise some people I have met. Police officers laugh, cry, vote, love, have families, pay bills and get frustrated just like other people. The difference is police officers cannot afford to dwell on most of these brain cluttering thoughts, or preoccupations, while on duty. The working patrol officer must discipline himself to avoid rearranging his family budget problems while walking or driving his beat.

Apathy, as stated earlier, is usually the insidious disease of indifference and disinterest suffered by cynical police officers. It is readily apparent and should be "attacked" and eliminated by good supervision and management. Two of the cases, those of Sergeant Adams and Officer Sam Reid, exhibited classic examples of apathy in motion. Unfortunately, but as is true in the usual case, their apathy led to the deaths of other police officers.

261

Clarence Kelley, in his "Message from the Director," in the February 1, 1974 issue of the *FBI Law Enforcement Bulletin,* indicates that there are many constructive countermeasures that could be taken to hold to a minimum the wanton killing of police officers: training, safer arrest techniques; intensified investigations to apprehend dangerous felons; better equipment; and high speed communications. Mr. Kelley then concludes:

> "But, even with all these safeguards, the stark fact remains that many law enforcement encounters—particularly during patrol—are unpredictable and explosively lethal to the officer. He must constantly remind himself that there is nothing routine in law enforcement duty. He cannot shirk that duty even when it—as it frequently does—propels him suddenly and without warning into the jaws of grave human conflict. At these dangerous times, an officer's only companion is his alertness."

Stay alert, stay alive.

glossary of terms

14

ADW   Assault with a deadly weapon

AI CAR   Traffic Accident Investigation Unit

AMBULANCE SHOOTING   A shooting with injuries or fatality; an ambulance is enroute Code 3

AMBULANCE TRAFFIC   A traffic accident with injuries or fatality; an ambulance is enroute Code 3

BAIT MONEY   Money in a bank teller's drawer that if removed from the drawer will trigger a robbery alarm

CCW   Carrying a concealed weapon

CODE 2   Urgent call; proceed immediately but without siren. Red (or blue) lights optional

CODE 3   Emergency call. Proceed immediately using red (or blue) lights and siren

CODE 4   No further assistance required

CODE 7   Time out to eat

COM' LINE   Communications or land line

DFAR Daily Field Activity Report. A log of activities kept by patrol officers

D.O.B. Date of Birth

DOUBLE OUGHT BUCK Shot, .32 caliber in size, commonly used in police shotguns

DUI Driving under the influence of alcohol

ETA Estimated time of arrival

F.I. Field interview, usually refers to the small 3"x5" card on which the F.I. is recorded

FIRE FIGHT An exchange of gunfire; a gun fight

GRASS Marijuana

HOT SHEET Card with a current list of stolen vehicles

NMI No middle initial

PPC Practical pistol course

PULL THE PIN To retire

REDS Secobarbital, or seconal. A quick-acting tranquilizer. A barbiturate

TAG Motor vehicle license plate

WAREX Heading on a police teletype indicating "WE HAVE A WARRANT AND WILL EXTRADITE"